180 Bible Verses for

DIFFICULT
TIMES

Carey Scott

180 Bible Verses for

DIFFICULT TIMES

Devotions for Women

BARBOUR
PUBLISHING

Published by Barbour Publishing, Inc., 1810 Barbour Drive, Uhrichsville, Ohio 44683, www.barbourbooks.com

Our mission is to inspire the world with the life-changing message of the Bible.

Member of the
Evangelical Christian
Publishers Association

Printed in China.

Introduction

The Bible is clear that our life here on earth will include challenges and struggles. There's no way around it. No chance to opt out. But as believers, we can have hope! Through scripture, we have access to God's life-changing words that will equip us. And no matter what we're facing, we'll find guidance and comfort every time we open His Word.

In the Bible's pages, you'll experience supernatural encouragement for those demanding moments. Your anxious heart will find peace. You'll be reminded of the power of God's constant presence in your life. And a renewed strength will rise up in you for the journey ahead.

Let the weighty words of God meet you in the hard places. When you cry out to Him for help, you're never alone. Friend, in the difficult, trust in the divine.

When You Keep Sin Hidden

Whoever tries to hide his sins will not
succeed, but the one who confesses his sins
and leaves them behind will find mercy.
PROVERBS 28:13 VOICE

. . . .

It's our natural response to want to hide our failures. We don't want others to see how we've made a mess of a situation. Because we're already experiencing shame, the last thing we want is for our blunder to be exposed and compound how bad we already feel. But our attempt to hide offenses only makes things worse. God has made a way to find freedom from the yucky feelings that accompany hidden sin, and it's through our honest and humble confession.

Are you craving compassion today? Are you desperate for a sense of relief from the shame you've been shouldering? Admit your hidden sins to God right now, and watch how He restores peace in your heart and joy in your day.

2

Hope Restored

When the righteous cry out, the LORD listens;
he delivers them from all their troubles.
The LORD is close to the brokenhearted;
he saves those whose spirits are crushed.

PSALM 34:17–18 CEB

. . . .

It's not hard to feel hopeless with all the world brings our way. From social stresses to financial frustrations to parenting problems, feeling discouraged can come easy. But it's what we choose to do with those feelings that makes the difference.

Friend, God has invited you to cry out to Him for help. No matter what it is, He is interested. And because you're a believer, the Lord promises to hear and deliver you from the burdens that are threatening to sink you. So be honest with God in your desperation, and let Him come close as He heals the crushed places that breed hopelessness. You are not alone, and restoration is on its way.

3

The Stress and Strife of Litigation

So now the case is closed. There remains no accusing voice of condemnation against those who are joined in life-union with Jesus, the Anointed One. For the "law" of the Spirit of life flowing through the anointing of Jesus has liberated us from the "law" of sin and death. For God achieved what the law was unable to accomplish, because the law was limited by the weakness of human nature.

ROMANS 8:1–3 TPT

• •

Condemnation no longer has power over your heart because of Jesus. Let this blessing be a constant companion in the courtroom too.

Being tangled in legal issues brings stress and strife, so let Jesus counter that with a calm to wash over your anxious heart. Let His words ring in your ears. Remember: He is with you always. And if you'll let Him, the Lord will steady you as you walk the process.

4

Loving Our Enemies

When your enemies fall, don't rejoice. When they stumble, don't let your heart be glad.

PROVERBS 24:17 CEB

. . . .

If honest, we'd admit to times when we wished our enemies the worst. Maybe we silently celebrated their fall or smirked over their failure. Maybe we pumped our fist in the air when they got what they deserved. Or maybe we giggled as their world imploded, glad they finally reaped what they sowed. But that grieves the heart of God.

If our heart was in the right place to begin with, it wouldn't be rejoicing at their demise. Enemies or not, we're to have compassion and love for everyone. Don't you know God has seen every interaction between us and them? He understands why our heart has been hurt. And when we give our pain to the Lord to heal, we're supernaturally enabled to treat others with kindness.

5

The Struggle to Forgive

But instead be kind and affectionate toward one another. Has God graciously forgiven you? Then graciously forgive one another in the depths of Christ's love.
EPHESIANS 4:32 TPT

- -

Sometimes it takes all we have to forgive, especially when our offenders are those we thought trustworthy. We worry extending grace tells them the hurt they caused wasn't a big deal. Instead, our choice to release them reveals a pursuit of righteous living. It removes any power their actions hold to keep us entangled. Forgiveness frees us from living offended, and it keeps our heart from becoming bitter and hard.

God's Word says to be kind and affectionate—something we cannot walk out when we hold a grudge. Today, talk to God about why it's hard to let go, and ask Him to give you courage to forgive so you can live with grace and thrive in community.

6

Using Words as Beautiful Gifts

And never let ugly or hateful words come from your mouth, but instead let your words become beautiful gifts that encourage others; do this by speaking words of grace to help them.
EPHESIANS 4:29 TPT

Many of us go for the jugular in arguments. Rather than unpack our feelings in heated yet respectful ways, we unleash the most hurtful and hateful words we can muster. Our goal is to knock them to their knees so we emerge the victor. Our rant is designed to put them in their place. And it's just terrible.

What if you approached arguments from a godly perspective? What if in the heat of the moment you silently asked God to let your next words be beautiful gifts rather than hurtful arrows? Ask the Lord for discernment and strength to stay quiet until you're able to speak words of grace.

7

Choosing Friends Wisely

Do not allow this world to mold you in its own image. Instead, be transformed from the inside out by renewing your mind. As a result, you will be able to discern what God wills and whatever God finds good, pleasing, and complete.
ROMANS 12:2 VOICE

. . . .

Be careful to choose friends who point you to God rather than to worldly pursuits. There's nothing to be gained by hanging out with people who prioritize fleshly desires. By pushing you in that direction, they're setting you up for failure. Their focus on the wrong things will eventually cause you to focus there too. It's inevitable.

Instead, let godly friendships be a priority. Find others who challenge you to rise up in faith for each moment you face. Surround yourself with a community that advocates for the kind of transformation and renewal that glorifies God. And choose to be that kind of friend too.

8

The Weight of Worry

Don't be pulled in different directions or worried about a thing. Be saturated in prayer throughout each day, offering your faith-filled requests before God with overflowing gratitude. Tell him every detail of your life, then God's wonderful peace that transcends human understanding, will guard your heart and mind through Jesus Christ.

PHILIPPIANS 4:6–7 TPT

- -

The key to living worry-free is being saturated in prayer. That may mean praying every morning or every minute of the day. You may go to God more times than you can count. But each time you redirect your thoughts to the Lord, you're training your heart to trust Him more than your anxiety.

It is possible to live without the weight of worry. You can thrive in wonderful peace. And you're the one who can make that happen by giving each worry to God, knowing it's in good hands.

9

The Destabilization of Job Loss

"I know what I'm doing. I have it all planned out—plans to take care of you, not abandon you, plans to give you the future you hope for."
JEREMIAH 29:11 MSG

. . . .

Few things can stir up stress more than losing a job, because it destabilizes you. Fear over finances comes bubbling to the top, causing peace to float away. As we forecast our future, we see only horrible outcomes and endings. That is, until we flex our faith.

The truth is God knows exactly what He's doing. He has everything planned out in a way that benefits you and glorifies Him. So no matter how scary it may feel, your best next move is to trust God. Let Him settle your anxious heart. Friend, He will take care of you! You're not alone. And your future is bright because He's already there.

10

The Valley of Chronic Illness

Even when your path takes me through the valley of deepest darkness, fear will never conquer me, for you already have! Your authority is my strength and my peace. The comfort of your love takes away my fear. I'll never be lonely, for you are near.

PSALM 23:4 TPT

. . . .

Chronic illness can lead to the valley of deepest darkness. Persistent pain and suffering require divine support every day. And it takes faith to replace the fear rising up in our heart. It's a good thing we have the great physician to hold us up.

These circumstances should drive us into the arms of God. We simply cannot navigate in our own strength. We need His peace and comfort. We need His love and presence. And when we cling to the Lord, He will lead us through the darkness with a sure and steady hand.

II

{ When You're a Victim of Violence }

*When I am afraid, I will put my
trust and faith in You.*
PSALM 56:3 AMP

. . . .

Being the victim of violence is a heartbreaking reality for many. Be it at the hands of a stranger or someone we deeply love, it shakes us to the core and leaves us feeling unsteady. Friend, we don't need to weather this storm alone. We need a community to bring support necessary to help us feel safe again. But most of all, we need God.

Scripture says He's our safe place. And because He knows every detail of the violence as well as the depths of your heart, God can minister to you in significant ways. You can trust Him to intervene. You can believe He is acting on your behalf. And you can have faith He will bring meaningful justice in the right ways and at the right time.

12

Trusting through Infertility

*"But blessed is the man who trusts me, GOD,
the woman who sticks with GOD. They're
like trees replanted in Eden, putting down
roots near the rivers—never a worry through
the hottest of summers, never dropping a
leaf, serene and calm through droughts,
bearing fresh fruit every season."*

JEREMIAH 17:7-8 MSG

In times like these all we can do is trust the Lord and His plan. So often there are no words from friends or family that will calm the deep longing you have for a child. No amount of hugs will change the pain you feel in the waiting. Even well-intentioned platitudes will leave you feeling empty and unseen. That's why the Word tells us to trust God for the nourishment our soul needs to feel refreshed.

Let God be your comforter. Let Him replenish hope. When you're thirsty for possibility, deepen your roots of faith in the one who can satisfy.

13

Nothing Is Hopeless

*I can do all things [which He has called me to
do] through Him who strengthens and empowers
me [to fulfill His purpose—I am self-sufficient
in Christ's sufficiency; I am ready for anything
and equal to anything through Him who infuses
me with inner strength and confident peace.]*

PHILIPPIANS 4:13 AMP

• •

With God's willingness to equip you with all good things
needed to do what He's asking, it's important to remember
nothing is hopeless. If your calling takes strength, He will
provide it. Does it require keen wisdom? You'll receive it.
When stepping out of your comfort zone is essential, God
will infuse you with courage, and you'll be given perseverance for the long road ahead.

Friend, God has your back. You are not alone in your
calling. Even more, you can be confident knowing you'll
receive everything you need for this next step in obedience.

14

Peace through Foreclosure

"You will keep in perfect and constant peace the one whose mind is steadfast [that is, committed and focused on You—in both inclination and character], because he trusts and takes refuge in You [with hope and confident expectation]."

ISAIAH 26:3 AMP

. . . .

Your biggest ally as you navigate the turmoil of foreclosure is God. He is the only one who can steady your heart and mind. When you're left to feel exposed, He will be your refuge. When you're confused about what to do next, God will guide your steps. And when you're beating yourself up and feeling like a failure, He'll bring a constant source of peace.

Be kind to yourself as you grieve the loss of your home. Ask God for a confident expectation for the future He's thoughtfully planned out. Let hope rise in your heart because you know God is good. . .all the time.

15

Why Failure Rocks Us

Now, may the Lord himself, the Lord of peace, pour into you his peace in every circumstance and in every possible way. The Lord's tangible presence be with you all.

2 THESSALONIANS 3:16 TPT

. . . .

Failure rocks us to the core because the enemy whispers in our ear, saying we're worthless. We carry the weight of shame, embarrassed by our missteps. And rather than extend grace to ourselves, we replay each mistake repeatedly. This isn't God's plan for you, friend. Instead, He wants to pour His peace into those messy moments so they lose their power to discourage your heart.

Let's keep in mind that perfection isn't the goal of our life. As humans, it's just not possible. And in a fallen world, it would never be sustainable. But in those very flawed moments, seek God's presence through the Word and time in prayer. That's how peace will prevail.

The Stress of Bankruptcy

So, what do you think? With God on our side like this, how can we lose? If God didn't hesitate to put everything on the line for us, embracing our condition and exposing himself to the worst by sending his own Son, is there anything else he wouldn't gladly and freely do for us?

ROMANS 8:31–32 MSG

• •

Not only is financial stress hard to navigate physically, it's also difficult emotionally. We feel we've let down those we love the most, and the guilt is almost too much to bear. It puts a kink in the way daily lives are lived, and we wonder how we'll make ends meet. Friend, those are valid feelings; but as believers, they aren't permanent ones.

God is right there with you. In the middle of the pain and confusion, He is by your side. He will do what's necessary to restore what's broken.

Purified from Sin's Pollution

*But if we own up to our sins, God shows
that He is faithful and just by forgiving us of
our sins and purifying us from the pollution
of all the bad things we have done.*

1 JOHN 1:9 VOICE

. . . .

There's a freedom that comes from owning up to your shortcomings and failures. Even more, scripture says doing so will purify you from the pollution they bring forth. And when you humbly confess hidden sin, it allows you to breathe easily rather than wheeze from its smog.

There's nothing you can do to make God love you any more or any less than He does right now. The truth is He already knows the sin you're trying so hard to cover. So when you confess, God clears the air between the two of you. Your lungs will fill with His goodness as you enjoy the fresh breezes of His faithfulness.

18

Chained to Unforgiveness

*Therefore, confess your sins to one another [your
false steps, your offenses], and pray for one
another, that you may be healed and restored.
The heartfelt and persistent prayer of a righteous
man (believer) can accomplish much [when put
into action and made effective by God—it is
dynamic and can have tremendous power].*

JAMES 5:16 AMP

• •

It takes mature faith to put aside hurt feelings and forgive.
Too often, we justify holding on to offenses and keeping
score. But if your goal is righteous living, then keeping
short accounts is essential. And once you confess and
forgive, commit to pray for one another, knowing it leads
to healing and restoration.

Life's too short to be chained to unforgiveness. It's
a prison with no escape route. Just as in other areas of
life, God has made a way to live in freedom—by humble
confession and willing forgiveness.

Staying Full of Faith with Financial Stress

*"This is why I tell you to never be worried about
your life, for all that you need will be provided,
such as food, water, clothing—everything your
body needs. Isn't there more to your life than
a meal? Isn't your body more than clothing?"*

MATTHEW 6:25 TPT

. . . .

If we find ourselves worried over finances, we are disobeying the Lord because He directly tells us to reject anxious thoughts. As a matter of fact, scripture says we are to *never* be worried about life. Whatever it is we need, God promises it will be provided at the right time. So spending any time worrying is a waste of time.

Staying full of faith during financial strain isn't easy. But when we drench ourselves in the Word and trust in His provision, we'll become rich in God's truth. And that will bring peace and comfort for the journey.

Trusting God in the Hopelessness

But those who trust in the Eternal One will regain their strength. They will soar on wings as eagles. They will run—never winded, never weary. They will walk—never tired, never faint.
ISAIAH 40:31 VOICE

· ·

Hold on, friend. When the urge to give up falls heavy on your heart, dig in. Stay engaged as you wait on God's help. The Bible is full of encouragement to trust the Lord, reminding each believer He is faithful to those who love Him. And when we choose to activate our own faith, scripture says we will regain strength for the battle. Even more, we'll have energy and perseverance to navigate it well.

Whatever has left you hopeless, turn your eyes upon Jesus. Let Him resuscitate and rejuvenate you so you're able to stand strong. When you choose to focus on the Lord to meet every need, your confidence will be rewarded.

21

Grieving as Your Parents Age

"At that time, you will call out for Me, and I will hear. You will pray, and I will listen. You will look for Me intently, and you will find Me."
JEREMIAH 29:12-13 VOICE

It's difficult to watch our once-spry parents begin to age. To see them struggling with basic activities is painful. And when roles reverse and we become the caretaker, it often creates a deep sadness. We miss who they've always been for us. We miss their ability to care in the ways they always have. And our heart becomes heavy.

Friend, you're not alone. God sees the changes and understands the complex emotions you are experiencing! So cry out to Him. Pour out your heartache and fears, because He is listening. Grieve in God's presence, trusting Him for comfort and peace. Every time you do, you'll find the strength for another day.

22

Why God Requires Forgiveness

Be even-tempered, content with second place, quick to forgive an offense. Forgive as quickly and completely as the Master forgave you. And regardless of what else you put on, wear love. It's your basic, all-purpose garment. Never be without it.

COLOSSIANS 3:13–14 MSG

• •

It's vital we keep short accounts with others. If we don't, we'll end up collecting offenses against those we love the most. The proverbial scorecard will ensure we keep our eyes on their wrongdoing rather than any kind of reconciliation. And we'll be miserable.

God requires forgiveness for your benefit, because it frees you up to love. And love opens the door to create community, which brings a sense of belonging. When we feel accepted by God and others, our confidence grows and our faith deepens. So choose to extend grace rather than hold on tightly to bitterness. Your happiness depends on it!

Don't Collect Enemies

*Pursue the goal of peace along with
everyone—and holiness as well, because
no one will see the Lord without it.*

HEBREWS 12:14 CEB

. . . .

If God has commanded us to live at peace with everyone, then how can we justify having enemies? It's often through harmonious living that others see the value of following the Lord. They witness our transformation. They watch us live unoffended. They recognize the ways we pursue peace. And through it all, they see God.

Be careful to not collect enemies. It's exhausting, if we are to be honest. And if our goal is to live a life that's righteous and pleasing to God, then we simply can't tag as enemies the ones who hurt or annoy us. We can set healthy boundaries, though, because He isn't asking us to be doormats. So choose peace, and let your life point to God—imperfectly but purposefully.

24

Call on the Fear Buster

*When I needed the Lord, I looked for Him;
I called out to Him, and He heard me and
responded. He came and rescued me from
everything that made me so afraid.*

PSALM 34:4 VOICE

God knew fear would be a big deal for believers. Maybe that's why He mentioned it over 350 times in His Word. The command to not fear is crystal clear, yet many of us still struggle. And for some, it's the lens through which they look at life. But don't forget the awesome power of God to make you courageous!

When you feel fear creeping in, pray. Right then and there, ask God for help. Candidly tell Him what scares you. That act of honesty will trigger His rescue. Scripture says God will save you from *everything* you fear. He won't ignore you, so trust Him. God's the best fear buster we've got.

25

Selfishness Ruins Relationships

People whose lives are based on selfishness think about selfish things, but people whose lives are based on the Spirit think about things that are related to the Spirit.

ROMANS 8:5 CEB

. . . .

Selfishness kills a good relationship. When people think only of themselves, it leaves no room for the feelings and needs of others. One becomes inconsequential because the focus is on the egotistical. And since relationships are a two-way street, one-way traffic shuts down anything meaningful. It's not sustainable if one desires deeper connections.

But when you love God's way, it opens the door to mutual care and compassion. Rather than looking out for number one, a servant's heart is cultivated. And the goal becomes improving the days of the ones you care about. It doesn't mean your relationships will be without stress and strife. But it does mean God will be glorified in the journey.

26

Alone in Sickness

My heart pounds; my strength abandons me. Even the light of my eyes is gone. My loved ones and friends keep their distance from me in my sickness; those who were near me now stay far away.

PSALM 38:10–11 CEB

· ·

If you're battling sickness right now, find comfort in knowing God sees you. He understands the valleys and mountaintops you're navigating, and He's with you. God hears your cries for companionship, and He never leaves your side. Even more, the Lord recognizes the intricacy of emotions stirring your spirit, and He will calm them when asked.

You're not expected to figure this out on your own. Even when you feel abandoned by your earthly support system, God's Spirit is with you always. You'll find strength through Him as your heart is comforted by His presence. And rest assured nothing will keep God away from His beloved.

When Family Feuds over Your Faith

*I am at peace and even take pleasure in any
weaknesses, insults, hardships, persecutions, and
afflictions for the sake of the Anointed because
when I am at my weakest, He makes me strong.*
2 CORINTHIANS 12:10 VOICE

The Bible clearly states we will be persecuted for our faith—and persecution can come in many different forms. From physical harm to discrimination to rude comments, chances are you will experience it, especially in the world today. But it's a whole new level of heartache when it comes from family.

There will be those who don't believe in what we believe in, and it will cause stress and strain. Those closest may reject us for following Jesus. They may hurl insults and make demands in an effort to change our minds. But in those times of weakness, ask God to strengthen your resolve to stand strong in faith.

28

Involving God in Our Challenges

Don't run from tests and hardships, brothers and sisters. As difficult as they are, you will ultimately find joy in them; if you embrace them, your faith will blossom under pressure and teach you true patience as you endure. And true patience brought on by endurance will equip you to complete the long journey and cross the finish line—mature, complete, and wanting nothing.

JAMES 1:2-4 VOICE

• •

Life is full of challenges! We're fallen people living in a fallen world, trying to navigate relationships with other fallen people. We will—we already have—face difficulties of all kinds. But let today's scripture remind you that if we involve God, He will bring beauty from these messy moments in unexpected ways.

So embrace the tests and hardships. Doing so will bring fuller faith, padded patience, and extended endurance, and these will bring you across the finish line lacking nothing.

29

When Alcohol Is Your God

*I believe that the present suffering is
nothing compared to the coming glory
that is going to be revealed to us.*
ROMANS 8:18 CEB

• •

In an effort to numb the pain, we often look for worldly
solutions to make our situation more tolerable. Our desire
is to quiet the negative voices, take away the guilt, cover
up the pain, or provide an escape route for a while. And
one of the go-to choices is alcohol. In that moment, we
are looking to it as we should be looking to God.

Scripture says we should have an eternal perspective,
understanding earthly suffering can't compare to our
heavenly freedom. It's challenging us to stay focused on
the coming glory rather than the current pain. And when
your heart and mind are anchored in the hope of eternity,
the things of this world grow strangely dim.

30

Saved from Toxic Friendships

Eternal One, do not leave me to their mercy; my True God, don't be far from me when they are near. I need Your help now—not later. O Lord, be my Rescuer.

PSALM 38:21-22 VOICE

. . . .

When a friendship turns toxic, sometimes we don't see it for a while. It slowly changes from life giving to joy draining. But other times we can nail down the exact moment it takes a turn for the worse. Our discerning spirit speaks up loud and clear. And we cry out for God's help right then and there, in the moment of revelation. We are desperate for the Lord's rescue.

While we are called to love others, we aren't called to stay in toxic relationships that bring hurt and harm. God wouldn't ask that of His beloved. Instead, He tells us to let Him be the Savior we need in the moments we need saved.

Obsessed with Our Enemies

*Brothers and sisters, don't waste your breath
complaining about one another. If you
judge others, you will be judged yourself.
Be very careful! You will face the one true
Judge who is right outside the door.*

JAMES 5:9 VOICE

. . . .

The problem with having enemies is we obsess about them. Hurtful interactions replay on loop in our mind. We unpack our frustration with others, complaining more often than we realize. We become critical as we look for the ways they're annoying, and then we analyze at every opportunity. And without notice, our days end up revolving around them.

Instead, the focus should be on glorifying God with our words and actions. Be good to yourself by giving every angry or bitter feeling to Him. It's too consuming to carry alone. And playing the role of judge will only hurt you in the end.

The Father's Arms

His massive arms are wrapped around you, protecting you. You can run under his covering of majesty and hide. His arms of faithfulness are a shield keeping you from harm. You will never worry about an attack of demonic forces at night nor have to fear a spirit of darkness coming against you.

PSALM 91:4-5 TPT

• •

There are moments we feel fragile, recognizing our vulnerability in new ways. We're exposed and afraid, and it's in these helpless times we crave the safety of our Father's arms. We want to be wrapped up tight and protected from the world. We want God to figure everything out for us as we stay shielded from harm.

Friend, let God be your place of safety when the overwhelming feelings of helplessness settle in. Run to the Father, who promises to wrap you up in His love and protection. With Him, you are secure.

Peace or Worry

*Peace I leave with you; My [own] peace I now
give and bequeath to you. Not as the world
gives do I give to you. Do not let your hearts
be troubled, neither let them be afraid. [Stop
allowing yourselves to be agitated and disturbed;
and do not permit yourselves to be fearful and
intimidated and cowardly and unsettled.]*

JOHN 14:27 AMPC

What are the causes of your worries today, friend?
Relationships? Finances? Parenting? Health? The future?
Every decision you make to off-load your worry to God
is a decision for peace. It's removing opportunities for
ongoing agitation and overwhelming intimidation. It's a
brave choice because you're activating faith over fear. And
God will honor it by covering you with His supernatural
peace—peace unmatched by the world's offerings.

Don't let your heart be troubled, because the Lord
is with you. Let Him settle your thoughts and comfort
your spirit.

Asking for Financial Wisdom

*If you don't have all the wisdom needed for
this journey, then all you have to do is ask God
for it; and God will grant all that you need. He
gives lavishly and never scolds you for asking.*
JAMES 1:5 VOICE

· ·

If you're struggling financially and not sure what to do,
ask God for wisdom. Ask for the mind to understand
your situation. Ask for guidance—be it His or someone He
brings to help. Tell God where you feel unsure or insecure.
Be honest about your confusion. Lay out your fears and
where you've failed. Share your heart, unpacking emotions
entangling you. Your Father wants to hear it all.

Today's verse offers two amazing promises when you
do. First, your request for wisdom will be fulfilled lavishly
and in full. And second, you won't ever be rebuked for it.
God's got you, friend.

35

When Their Hidden Sin Affects You

*He's the hope that holds me and the stronghold
to shelter me, the only God for me, and my
great confidence. He will rescue you from every
hidden trap of the enemy, and he will protect you
from false accusation and any deadly curse.*

PSALM 91:2–3 TPT

• •

Sometimes you are the one with hidden sin that needs
to be revealed and healed. But other times it's you who
must walk out the natural consequences of someone else's
secreted wrongdoings. Maybe his betrayal led to divorce.
Maybe their financial choices caused bankruptcy. Maybe
her habits brought your parenting skills into question. Let
God be your only stronghold of shelter.

When scripture says He'll rescue you from the enemy's
hidden traps, it's guaranteed. When it says God will protect
you from wrongful blame, it's a promise. You may feel the
heat, but the flames won't torch you.

36

When You Don't Have the Words

*In the same way, the Spirit comes to help
our weakness. We don't know what we
should pray, but the Spirit himself pleads
our case with unexpressed groans.*

ROMANS 8:26 CEB

. . . .

Do you ever struggle to pray when you're overwhelmed by life? Maybe you're not sure what you're feeling inside, and that's causing uncertainty about what to ask. Maybe you can't find the words in the moment. Or maybe your circumstance has reduced you to tears and all you can do is groan from the heartache. When your prayers feel weak, trust the Holy Spirit to make every need known to God.

Your fragility doesn't intimidate the Lord or frustrate Him. Those moments of weakness only warm God's heart toward you. So don't wait to pray until you clean yourself up. The Holy Spirit is advocating on your behalf to a Father who loves you unconditionally.

37

Surrendering Anxiety

*Surrender your anxiety. Be still and realize that
I am God. I am God above all the nations, and
I am exalted throughout the whole earth.*
PSALM 46:10 TPT

. . . .

When you're anxious, it takes a great effort to be still.
Most often, stress spurs us into action, and we busily try
to control the situation at hand. And even when anxiety
paralyzes us, our mind is running ninety miles an hour.
There is no peace when our heart is anxious.

Why not surrender it? Why not take Him at His word,
stepping back so God can be God? We can spin ourselves
into a tizzy trying to manage everything within the limits
of our humanity. But the Lord's divine nature can bring
rest to us as He aligns all things with His perfect peace.
We don't need to be god, because the only true God is
already working on our behalf.

38

The Winds of Doubt

And Jesus said, "Come." Then Peter got out of the boat and was walking on the water toward Jesus. But when Peter saw the strong wind, he became frightened. As he began to sink, he shouted, "Lord, rescue me!" Jesus immediately reached out and grabbed him, saying, "You man of weak faith! Why did you begin to have doubts?"

MATTHEW 14:29–31 CEB

To doubt is to be human. Even if we love the Lord and our desire is to trust Him in all things, doubt can whoosh onto the scene in seconds flat.

Peter was able to walk on water. Literally. But once the winds began to gust, his focus moved from Jesus to the turbulence. He doubted the divine, and it sank him. When adversity blows into your day, you can be unshakable in faith or uncertain in fear. The choice is yours to make.

Depressed because of Aging Bodies

So we aren't depressed. But even if our bodies
are breaking down on the outside, the person
that we are on the inside is being renewed
every day. Our temporary minor problems
are producing an eternal stockpile of glory
for us that is beyond all comparison.

2 CORINTHIANS 4:16–17 CEB

. . . .

Have you heard the saying "Aging ain't for the weak of heart"? It can be difficult to see our youthfulness disappear. It's hard to embrace the aches and pains. And it's depressing to experience the breakdown of our bodies. But consider this a temporary, minor problem!

When we see Jesus, we will have a new and improved glorified body, able to move and shake with the best of them. It won't break down or give in to disease. It won't wrinkle or wear out. Keeping that kind of eternal perspective will replace depression with delight!

40

The Gift of God's Kindness

You know we call those blessed [happy,
spiritually prosperous, favored by God]
who were steadfast and endured [difficult
circumstances]. You have heard of the patient
endurance of Job and you have seen the Lord's
outcome [how He richly blessed Job]. The
Lord is full of compassion and is merciful.

JAMES 5:11 AMP

Since the Lord is full of compassion, as believers we'll be able to experience it. We will feel His kindness as we journey through sickness. He will send us a community of care to minister to our heart and meet our physical needs. And as we stay close to Him, God will bring His favor to rest on us each day.

With spiritual eyes, you'll see the blessing. Your faith will allow you to have patient endurance like Job. Are you walking through a difficult health situation? Then expect His kindness in meaningful ways.

Seeking God through Divorce

*"So above all, constantly seek God's kingdom
and his righteousness, then all these less
important things will be given to you abundantly.
Refuse to worry about tomorrow, but deal with
each challenge that comes your way, one day
at a time. Tomorrow will take care of itself."*

MATTHEW 6:33–34 TPT

There's no doubt about it: the tearing apart of a family causes tragedy and destruction. And with a broken heart often comes a flood of worry and fear and anxiety. But God's timely encouragement is to seek Him above all else as you stay present in today. Looking to the world for answers is an empty well. Even more, looking ahead will only bring stress.

So let the Lord have your weariness and worry. Choose to let Him guide your path. And trust that your faith will unlock His goodness and provision each step of the way.

42

From Disappointment to Delightful

*We know that God works all things together
for good for the ones who love God, for those
who are called according to his purpose.*
ROMANS 8:28 CEB

. . . .

As believers, we can know that each disappointment is being knitted together into God's perfect design for us. He wastes nothing. And that should be an encouragement for many reasons, especially realizing God is fully aware of every celebration and challenge we face. He takes painful moments and brings about beauty. He takes each difficulty and creates something wonderful. And our heartaches are recycled into a blessing.

Take heart, friend! God hasn't missed one detail of your discouragement. He understands every factor leading up to your frustration. So ask God to open your eyes to see how He will turn each disappointment into something delightful and decent. . .always in His perfect timing and His amazing ways.

seenso
43

The Storm of Workplace Stress

*Keep trusting in the Lord and do what
is right in his eyes. Fix your heart on the
promises of God, and you will dwell in the
land, feasting on his faithfulness. Find your
delight and true pleasure in Yahweh, and he
will give you what you desire the most.*

PSALM 37:3-4 TPT

. . . .

When it comes to stress in the workplace, fixing your heart on God guarantees you a level of peace that will guide you through each day. The truth is man will always let you down. A job well done is often subjective. And when facing instability at the office, trusting God will help you stay humble and honorable as you navigate the ever-changing path.

Let your delight be found in your relationship with the Lord. Pour into it daily. Spend time in the Word and in prayer. Follow His will and ways. And watch as you weather the storm in peace.

Preparing to Face Death

The grass withers, the flower fades as the breath of the Eternal One blows away. People are no different from grass. The grass withers, the flower fades; nothing lasts except the word of our God. It will stand forever.

ISAIAH 40:7-8 VOICE

. . . .

We will eventually face death—either our own or that of someone we deeply love. And while the reality of it can bring sadness and fear, if we are believers, we can stand in faithful confidence that death is not the end. Our last breath here leads to our first breath in heaven.

As you're preparing to face death, let this be a prayerful season. Spend time on this side of eternity praising God for His faithfulness. Thank Him for the promise of heaven. Open the Word and relish the verses that have sustained you in hard times. And let God bring comfort and peace.

When Our Identity Is Involved

*Pour out all your worries and stress
upon him and leave them there, for he
always tenderly cares for you.*

1 PETER 5:7 TPT

. . . .

Why do we clutch our worries? Why do we cling to stress?
Why do we cleave to anxiety and fear? God has lovingly
offered to take them all—every one of them. He promises
to relieve us of duty. But too often, we won't give them up.
Are we getting something in return?

Some misguidedly embrace their identity of being a
hot mess. It brings desired attention, and they reap the
benefits of always being in a state of chaos. But we aren't
victims. As believers, we are instead victors because God
offers to remove any burden that keeps us messy. If you're
unwilling to give Him your worries, ask the Lord to reveal
what's really going on.

46

When You Need Strength in Loss

The moment I called out, you stepped in;
you made my life large with strength.
PSALM 138:3 MSG

. . . .

What a blessing to know that our cries to the Lord are met with an infusion of strength, especially as we navigate the rocky road of losing a parent. Even if the passing was expected and the end to long suffering, the death leaves a hole in our heart that only God can fill.

Take every moment of pain directly to the one who will step in without hesitation. With an expectant heart, tell Him what you need throughout the process. Ask God for supernatural strength and endurance to walk this season out through faith. Trust Him to step in with you. And then watch as God makes your "life large" with every good thing. You're not alone, friend.

47

When Panic Causes Doubt

Yes, God is more than ready to overwhelm you with every form of grace, so that you will have more than enough of everything—every moment and in every way. He will make you overflow with abundance in every good thing you do.

2 CORINTHIANS 9:8 TPT

When we're panicking, it's all too common for us to doubt God will show up. Chances are we have a robust testimony of times He intervened in our life, but current circumstances have us flustered and frightened. We question if God will show up once again.

Scripture says God is ready. In His compassion, He's prepared to cover you with all you need—and then some. You will receive everything to navigate every moment in every way necessary. So rather than allow panic to cause doubt, activate your faith to believe God's promise to equip.

Nothing Can Separate

*I'm convinced that nothing can separate us
from God's love in Christ Jesus our Lord: not
death or life, not angels or rulers, not present
things or future things, not powers or height
or depth, or any other thing that is created.*

ROMANS 8:38–39 CEB

Few things can knock us to our knees like the sting of sexual betrayal. It hits a deep place of pain, causing us to hemorrhage in ways we never knew possible. Whether you're the one caught in adultery or it was your husband, this moral failure is laced with shame. And it often feels as if it's destroyed your relationship with God.

Don't let that lie settle into your spirit. There's no room for it when the truth stands strong in your heart. Today's scripture reiterates that truth without mincing words. So confess. Repent. Forgive. And let God love you through restoration.

49

Supporting Others in the Death of a Pet

*Celebrate with those who celebrate,
and weep with those who grieve.*
ROMANS 12:15 TPT

. . . .

The best thing we can do for those grieving the loss of a furry friend is grieve with them. Losing a pet is a traumatic experience because they've been an integral part of life and family. They bring joy in the right ways and comfort at the right time. So saying goodbye ushers in a heartache only God and time can heal.

We don't need to fix the situation or find the perfect words to encourage their heart. We don't need to try to distract them. Instead, we need to follow their emotional lead. If their desire is to celebrate, join in. Or if they need to cry and talk about their beloved pet, do the same. Be the kind of person who supports however necessary.

Praying over Your Health

*Beloved, I pray that in every way you
may succeed and prosper and be in
good health [physically], just as [I know]
your soul prospers [spiritually].*

3 JOHN 2 AMP

. . . .

Do you pray specifically for good health? Sometimes we're
so lost in the illness at hand that we forget to talk to God
about it. So let today's verse be a reminder that prayers
for health are important. The truth is that whatever is on
your mind—whatever struggles you're facing—God wants
to hear about it.

Be specific. Be honest. Be real about your worries and
fears. Ask for the right doctors and nursing staff. Let God
lead you to the best medical facilities. Tell Him you trust
His treatment oversight. Ask for faith-filled caretakers with
wisdom and compassion. Ask for God's healing hand to
move in your body. And praise Him for being the great
physician!

The Battle with Insomnia

*So listen to what I'm saying: Whatever
you pray for or ask from God, believe
that you'll receive it and you will.*
MARK 11:24 VOICE

• •

Sleep is essential to your body for many reasons, but sometimes it eludes us. It may be a diagnosed medical condition, a physical reaction to food or drink, or related to personal stress. Regardless, nighttime is when our body refuses to shut down so we can sleep. And there seems to be nothing more we can do.

Use this time to pray for God to intervene. Share your frustrations and concerns. Open up about the toll it's taking on your productivity during the day. Ask God to bring your body into alignment with His will so you'll feel rested and rejuvenated each morning. And remember that if you ask in faith, believing He will bless your request, the Lord will honor it.

The Unmatched Comfort of God

If your faith remains strong, even while surrounded by life's difficulties, you will continue to experience the untold blessings of God! True happiness comes as you pass the test with faith, and receive the victorious crown of life promised to every lover of God!

JAMES 1:12 TPT

There's no quick or easy way to wade through the emotions of losing a child. Their death feels unnatural. Ill-timed. Unreconcilable. Yet for many, it's a reality we must face. Also for many, it shakes our faith to the core, begging the *Why, God?* questions.

Everyone's journey looks different, but one truth remains the same. When you cling to God through it rather than kick Him to the curb in anger, there will be unexpected and meaningful blessings. Every time you cry to Him in the heartache, God will meet you there. Let Him provide unmatched comfort as you grieve.

A Courageous Confidence

*So we will never fear even if every structure
of support were to crumble away. We will not
fear even when the earth quakes and shakes,
moving mountains and casting them into the
sea. For the raging roar of stormy winds and
crashing waves cannot erode our faith in you.*

PSALM 46:2–3 TPT

There are lots of scary situations facing us every day. We fear what the future may hold for our children. We worry the disease will return. We're afraid we won't be able to pay bills. And we're concerned about the state of the world. Friend, only God can calm an anxious heart.

Faith allows us to have courageous confidence. We may not know how He'll fix things, but we know He will. And when we trust God with what we fear—firmly believing He is able and willing—a bold belief will rise up and steady us.

54

The Stress of Family

*Whenever I walk into trouble, You are there
to bring me out. You hold out Your hand to
protect me against the wrath of my enemies,
and hold me safely in Your right hand.*

PSALM 138:7 VOICE

· ·

Many people spell *family* this way: STRESS. For a million reasons, being together can make you come undone. Why? Because we have history that often complicates gatherings. There are opposing ideas and views that spark arguments. And because of familiarity, we feel the freedom to speak our mind without reserve. The result is a kaboom!

Before your next roundup, make sure you're prayed up. God wants to set your heart right so you can bring compassion rather than chaos. And if the battle ensues, He'll also be the one to protect you and keep you steady. When you're facing the stress of family, find comfort in the safety of the Father.

Craving a Knight in Shining Armor

God, you're such a safe and powerful place to find refuge! You're a proven help in time of trouble—more than enough and always available whenever I need you.

PSALM 46:1 TPT

. . . .

When feeling helpless, many long for a knight in shining armor to ride in on a white horse and save the day. We crave a rescue from the oppression. We pine for a place of rest where we can feel protected from the storm. And we beg for a proven warrior to battle on our behalf. But friend, don't you know God is already all of these things *and more*?

He is everything we need and is available every time we need it. There's no reason to allow helplessness to rob us of joy and peace. Our weary heart will be strengthened! Once again, God has taken care of everything.

His Presence Overcomes Fear

*He is ever present with me; at all times He goes
before me. I will not live in fear or abandon my
calling because He stands at my right hand.*
PSALM 16:8 VOICE

It's because of God's presence that fear has no power over
us. He is the reason we can have confidence that things
will be okay. He is why courage courses through our veins,
giving us the ability to stand up for ourselves. It's God with
us who replaces our weakness with His strength. But it's
also a mindset we must choose each day.

Unless we do, we'll live under fear's dictatorship. It will
drive our decisions and skew our perspective. Our words
and actions will become ineffective for the kingdom. And
our lives won't model the faith we claim to have. Friend,
fear not, for God is with you at all times.

How to Slow Down Anger

*My dearest brothers and sisters, take this
to heart: Be quick to listen, but slow to
speak. And be slow to become angry, for
human anger is never a legitimate tool
to promote God's righteous purpose.*
JAMES 1:19–20 TPT

. . . .

Can we admit it's almost humanly impossible to slow
anger once it ignites? It takes off quickly and gets us into
trouble before we realize what's happened. We say hurtful words. We make unnecessary declarations. We spew
hateful comments we have worked hard to keep tucked
away. And our anger hurts not only others but also our
testimony of faith.

Let this reality drive you to grow in your relationship
with God. The more time you spend with Him, the more
His ways become yours. For many of us, it's only through
the Lord's strength that we can be quicker to listen and
slower to anger.

But God Sees the Heart

But the LORD said to Samuel, "Have no regard for his appearance or stature, because I haven't selected him. God doesn't look at things like humans do. Humans see only what is visible to the eyes, but the LORD sees into the heart."

1 SAMUEL 16:7 CEB

. . . .

There are times when surgery alters our appearance. Whether it's a known outcome or an unexpected result, it can leave us with deep insecurity. Why wouldn't it? This world places a premium on the outside of a person. But God does not.

Let's be grateful He included scripture like today's, because it connects deeply with a woman's heart. The world's ideals are often cruel and difficult to meet. But to know God doesn't see our value in the ways society does brings comfort. To the Lord, your heart is what makes you beautiful.

59

The Fountain of Hope

*Now may God, the fountain of hope, fill you to
overflowing with uncontainable joy and perfect
peace as you trust in him. And may the power of
the Holy Spirit continually surround your life with
his super-abundance until you radiate with hope!*

ROMANS 15:13 TPT

. . . .

God is called a fountain of hope in scripture. And it's
from this fountain that we're able to experience joy and
peace overflowing. When we trust Him, these are direct
blessings to believers. And it's a supernatural exchange we
can't explain. Partaking from the fountain of hope creates
a confident expectation.

So because we follow God and He is hope, hopelessness cannot live within us. We might feel discouraged or
downcast, but they can't stick. Gloomy feelings will be
short-lived. Misery will pass. We have the beautiful opportunity to drink from the fountain and have hope restored.

The Role of Angels

*God sends angels with special orders to
protect you wherever you go, defending you
from all harm. If you walk into a trap, they'll be
there for you and keep you from stumbling.*
PSALM 91:11–12 TPT

• •

Heavenly angels are with you always. They're acting on special orders from God, defending and protecting you from enemy plans full of evil intent. They're not to be worshipped or made godlike, but instead let them bring comfort. Your Father has thought of everything, and your protection is central.

While we may find ourselves in difficult places and violent spaces at times, it's important to remember God knows all. He allows these occurrences only because He sees the bigger picture full of plans for your good and His glory. And anything that would bring the opposite must face His angels, who are there to keep you from stumbling.

Temptation or Testing

Let no one say when he is tempted, "I am being tempted by God" [for temptation does not originate from God, but from our own flaws]; for God cannot be tempted by [what is] evil, and He Himself tempts no one.

JAMES 1:13 AMP

. . . .

Temptation and testing are not the same, and if we don't understand what sets them apart, it will bring confusion every time. The Bible is clear that when we're tempted to do things unpleasing to God, it's not from Him. He won't tempt us into sinning. But the Lord will test us to prove our faith genuine, grow our character as believers, and purify us.

That means any addiction we fall into isn't from God because it leads to sin. It's a form of idolatry because we desire something greater than Him. And if we ask in humility, He will deliver us from the stronghold addiction brings.

Not Crushed by Challenges

*We are experiencing all kinds of trouble,
but we aren't crushed. We are confused,
but we aren't depressed. We are harassed,
but we aren't abandoned. We are knocked
down, but we aren't knocked out.*

2 CORINTHIANS 4:8-9 CEB

. . . .

Life has a special way of punching us right in the gut. Amen? Daily, we're up against tough situations that feel overwhelming. From worrying about financial strains to fearing repercussions for standing up for your faith to navigating betrayal from someone you trusted, we are big-time challenged to stay peaceful and joyful.

What a relief to remember that as believers, our troubles can't crush us. We may not always have the answers, but we won't live without hope. Even when we feel picked on, God promises to stick with us. And nothing has the power to take us out. Flex your faith and stand in it.

Accepting the Flawed Church

"Are you tired? Worn out? Burned out on religion? Come to me. Get away with me and you'll recover your life. I'll show you how to take a real rest. Walk with me and work with me—watch how I do it. Learn the unforced rhythms of grace. I won't lay anything heavy or ill-fitting on you. Keep company with me and you'll learn to live freely and lightly."

MATTHEW 11:28-30 MSG

• •

Our churches are imperfect buildings full of imperfect people. Expecting anything more is a setup for failure. There may be good intentions and pure hearts, but church discord is a reality many face. Too often, we expect flawlessness from believers that isn't realistic or fair. God's people may not be perfect, but He is.

Choose to accept the church as flawed. It will allow you to be in community, together praising a flawless God.

64

How a Good Word Helps

The weight of worry drags us down,
but a good word lightens our day.
PROVERBS 12:25 VOICE

· ·

If you or someone you love has been in an accident, you know firsthand the worry that comes along with it. From the initial shock to the ongoing pain or doctor visits, there is a level of stress that becomes the undertow of each day. And no matter how much you try to find peace, it eludes you.

Sometimes what we need is a good word, because words matter. They have power. And whether it's from the Bible or encouragement from a friend, scripture says a "good word" lightens the load. So if you're the one who needs it, meditate on your favorite passage of scripture. And if someone else needs it, be the one who shares the perfect words to bring hope to a weary heart, if only for a while.

Content Even through Financial Stress

Yahweh is my best friend and my shepherd.
I always have more than enough.
PSALM 23:1 TPT

. . . .

Consider the key ingredient that made the psalmist feel deep contentment. It wasn't a bigger bank account. It wasn't a higher-paying job or hopes for a lucrative inheritance. Instead, it was God's presence. He recognized that because he trusted the Lord's provision, he wasn't lacking. He had more than enough.

Financial stress makes us hypervigilant about not having what we think we need. Even more, it plants fear that our livelihood will soon crash and burn. It forces us to focus on our deficiencies rather than recognize the fullness we have as believers. And all we see is what's missing. Friend, let your heart find rest knowing God is with you and will provide. Ask for contentment, and He will settle your spirit.

Praising through Difficulties

I will praise the Eternal in every moment
through every situation. Whenever I speak,
my words will always praise Him.
PSALM 34:1 VOICE

. . . .

A posture of praise makes every difficult moment doable. Why? Because it takes our eyes off the hard circumstances and refocuses them on the only one who can bring peace in their midst. And when we choose to worship and honor the Lord, we find the comfort we need as we're facing death.

We can rejoice that we'll see Him soon. We can celebrate the gift of salvation that guarantees eternal life. We can glorify God's name for being a constant companion through the process of dying. We can thank Him for the ways He blessed our life on earth through family and friends. We can praise the Lord that death is not final. So let your final days on earth be full of thanksgiving.

When We Overreact to Family Feuds

Love never brings fear, for fear is always related to punishment. But love's perfection drives the fear of punishment far from our hearts. Whoever walks constantly afraid of punishment has not reached love's perfection.

1 JOHN 4:18 TPT

. . . .

Sometimes family feuds stimulate a fear response that shuts us down. We feel destabilized, worried about retribution or rejection. We obsess over the ways we might be punished for speaking up and sharing our heart. And we beat ourselves up for letting our guard down. But are we overreacting?

Fighting doesn't automatically mean bad things are coming. Arguments are often healthy ways to figure things out. It's possible to deeply love and deeply feud at the same time. So don't let heated discussions cause you to spiral into discouragement. Ask God to make you confident of your family's love even when things feel messy.

Overcoming with God's Help

Whenever I feel my foot slipping, your faithful love steadies me, LORD. When my anxieties multiply, your comforting calms me down.
PSALM 94:18–19 CEB

. . . .

Drug abuse is a complex issue that often requires professional help to overcome. Anyone serious about living clean must face the triggers that drove them to drugs in the first place. And when you involve God in the process—asking for insight, revelation, and healing—He will be present.

That means every time you feel resolve slipping, the Lord will be there to steady you. He will fill you with courage and strength to stand firm in your decision to say no. When anxiety multiplies because your body is craving a fix, God will calm the frayed edges of your nerves. You will still have to choose rightly, but you won't be alone. Trust His help to overcome the abuse and align your heart with His.

Navigating the Prodigal Child

Do not let your hearts be troubled (distressed,
agitated). You believe in and adhere to and
trust in and rely on God; believe in and
adhere to and trust in and rely also on Me.

JOHN 14:1 AMPC

- -

As parents, it's imperative we trust God with our kids. When they walk away from all we've taught them, we can trust they're on God's radar. We don't have to live in anxiety, because He is working all things for their good. And even when it looks bleak, we can choose to believe in God's perfect ways and timing. He loves them more than we ever could, and His hand is on their life.

So ask God to steady your anxious and agitated heart. Ask Him to bring comfort, hope, and peace. And let the Lord anchor your faith deeper as you rest in His promises.

Maybe It's His Plan

You can be sure that God will take care of everything you need, his generosity exceeding even yours in the glory that pours from Jesus. Our God and Father abounds in glory that just pours out into eternity. Yes.

PHILIPPIANS 4:19–20 MSG

God will take care of it. Whatever needs you have right now, He knows them all. And your job loss doesn't interfere with His compassionate plans for your life one bit. Maybe it was His plan all along.

Sometimes we're reluctant to make the changes God is wanting because they are scary. It would require radical faith and a giant step out of our comfort zone. So consider there may be times the Lord must step in, giving you a loving nudge. Today, believe in God's provision, choose to trust His plan, and have bold faith in His promises!

When Worry Keeps Your Awake

*"So, which one of you by worrying
could add anything to your life?"*
MATTHEW 6:27 TPT

. . . .

What's keeping you awake? What are the stresses of the day that are wreaking havoc on your night? It can be so frustrating to start the morning exhausted, especially when your schedule is packed from start to end. But maybe there's a divine cure for your insomnia.

God is very clear about the issue of worrying. It's not something we're to carry, because it does nothing to help the situation. So in His great compassion, He offers to take it upon Himself. Why not give it to God throughout the day as it comes up? Be it ten times or one hundred, refuse to carry it yourself. That act of faith and surrender will help you sleep. Knowing it's in God's capable hands will allow you to rest.

For Your Good and His Glory

The Eternal will finish what He started in me.
Your faithful love, O Eternal One, lasts forever;
do not give up on what Your hands have made.

PSALM 138:8 VOICE

- -

When faced with difficult circumstances, we need to remember God is ever present and always working on our behalf. He may be growing our confidence through these hard times. He might be teaching us to persevere or endure. Maybe God is creating strength of character. Maybe He's making us more compassionate or generous. Regardless, we can trust that the Lord won't quit His perfecting work.

So when you're faced with challenges, take heart! God has allowed them for a good reason, and you are being held tightly in His hands as you wade through. Even more, the Lord will use them for your benefit and His glory.

Letting Vengeance Be His

*Beloved, don't be obsessed with taking
revenge, but leave that to God's righteous
justice. For the Scriptures say: "Vengeance
is mine, and I will repay," says the Lord.*
Romans 12:19 tpt

. . . .

The only true option we have as believers is to forgive.
Recognizing what God's forgiveness did for us as sinners,
we simply cannot justify holding on to bitterness toward
others. How can we not forgive, when we were so graciously
forgiven? It's our heart of gratitude for Jesus that prompts
us to extend grace.

Of course we want our offenders to pay. We may even
want them to feel our wrath in calculated and creative
ways. But your Father in heaven wants vengeance to
be His alone. God wants your heart freed from the bond-
age of unforgiveness. So ask Him to help you release the
burden into His hands, choosing to live unoffended and
full of grace.

Your Shield of Protection

For here is what the Lord has spoken to me:
"Because you loved me, delighted in me, and
have been loyal to my name, I will greatly protect
you. I will answer your cry for help every time you
pray, and you will feel my presence in your time
of trouble. I will deliver you and bring you honor."
PSALM 91:14–15 TPT

. . . .

Your faith acts as a shield of protection. Every time you demonstrate your love, delight, and loyalty to Him, the Lord's response is more of His presence. So when you cry out in times of trouble—times of abusiveness—you can be assured He will answer.

The Lord doesn't condone abuse. For believers, God promises to intervene. It may not be in the moment or in ways you prayed for, but deliverance will happen as you trust Him. Follow God's leading as He navigates you to a safer place.

Leaving Worries at His Feet Instead

*So here's what I've learned through it all: Leave
all your cares and anxieties at the feet of the
Lord, and measureless grace will strengthen you.*

PSALM 55:22 TPT

· ·

While most of the world will find themselves drowning in worry and anxiety, as believers we don't have to. It's not up to us to figure everything out. We don't have to have all the answers. And circling the mountain of stress over and over again doesn't make matters any better. As a matter of fact, it robs us of living with passion and purpose because we're always stirred up and focused on ourselves.

Every time you choose to place your cares at the Lord's feet, there will be a supernatural grace that brings strength. The worries won't own you any longer, and you'll find peace as you watch God make everything right.

The Frustration of Injustice

And let the peace (soul harmony which comes) from Christ rule (act as umpire continually) in your hearts [deciding and settling with finality all questions that arise in your minds, in that peaceful state] to which as [members of Christ's] one body you were also called [to live]. And be thankful (appreciative), [giving praise to God always].

Colossians 3:15 ampc

. . . .

Injustice is a hard pill to swallow for many because we choose to live according to God's commands, which are just and fair. But the world follows a whole different set of rules. Their idea of right and wrong can differ drastically from what God says. And we find ourselves stuck between the ideas of the earthly and the ideals of the eternal.

Ask God to fill your heart with peace, knowing He will eventually make right all that is wrong. Yes, you can trust Him to do so.

The Way We Hope and Endure

*Whatever was written beforehand is meant to
instruct us in how to live. The Scriptures impart
to us encouragement and inspiration so that
we can live in hope and endure all things.*

ROMANS 15:4 TPT

• •

When your chronic pain feels too overwhelming, open
up God's Word. There is a magical sense to it because it's
God-breathed. Every word was included for a reason. So
when you take the time to read from the Bible, it can't help
but bring inspiration. No matter how discouraged you feel,
digging into scripture will boost your spirit.

Let yourself find hope in its pages. It may not take
away the pain that nags you daily, but it will shift your
mind and give you fresh perspective. Even more, you'll find
the strength to endure the difficult path you are having
to walk each day.

Why We Can Hope for Change

"For with God nothing [is or ever] shall be impossible."

LUKE 1:37 AMP

• •

Sometimes we need to know there is a possibility. We need to know there's hope for something better. Our heart cries out to be encouraged that things can change. And knowing that God is in the business of miracle moments, we can be reassured that healing of an addiction can be a reality. His Word says *nothing* is impossible.

Be it something you're struggling with or the battle for someone you deeply love, don't lose heart when it comes to defeating addiction. Never give up hope for recovery. The road may be long and steep and rocky, but your Father says restoration is possible. Let God grow your faith by pressing into Him for help. He hears you. He loves you. And God will work all things for good when you trust.

The Pain of Disloyalty
and Unfaithfulness

*Tell those who worry, the anxious and fearful,
"Take strength; have courage! There's nothing
to fear. Look, here—your God! Right here is your
God! The balance is shifting; God will right
all wrongs. None other than God will give you
success. He is coming to make you safe."*

ISAIAH 35:4 VOICE

• •

What a gift for us to read in His Word that God will right all
wrongs. In His infinite wisdom, He will shift the balance at
the right time and in the right ways. And those who have
betrayed us will answer to the Lord.

The pain that comes from disloyalty and unfaithfulness
is almost unbearable because it's unexpected. It shocks
us to the core. Even more, it often comes from those we
trusted the most. But scripture says we're to take strength
and have courage because God is on the move.

You're Not an Accident

For You shaped me, inside and out. You knitted me together in my mother's womb long before I took my first breath. I will offer You my grateful heart, for I am Your unique creation, filled with wonder and awe. You have approached even the smallest details with excellence; Your works are wonderful; I carry this knowledge deep within my soul.

PSALM 139:13-14 VOICE

Friend, you're not an accident. God made you *on* purpose and *for* a purpose. He knitted you together with love and care. And He took His time, delighted in who He made you to be. God wasn't in a bad mood or rushed when you were formed.

Don't partner with enemy lies telling you differently. You're here by design. And even more, the heavens celebrated the day you took your first breath. No, you are most certainly not an accident. Instead, you're the beloved daughter of the King.

Overwhelmed by Disabilities

He offers a resting place for me in his
luxurious love. His tracks take me to an oasis
of peace near the quiet brook of bliss. That's
where he restores and revives my life. He
opens before me the right path and leads
me along in his footsteps of righteousness
so that I can bring honor to his name.

PSALM 23:2–3 TPT

While we learn to navigate life with disabilities, there are times it feels overwhelming. There are moments we wish things were different. And when we focus on it too much, it can bring chaos to our heart. Then we collide with today's verses, and we see God's unmatched love.

Be comforted in knowing there's a resting place. . .an oasis of peace. . .and a quiet brook of bliss in the Lord's presence. It's there we're revived. Let God meet you in your weakness and strengthen you for the day.

82

When You're Treated Badly

The wicked gang up against the lives of the righteous. They condemn innocent blood. But the LORD is my fortress; my God is my rock of refuge.

PSALM 94:21-22 CEB

. . . .

The reality is there's much wickedness and evil in the world, and it's guaranteed our paths will cross it from time to time. We will encounter abuse and cruelty regardless of our best-laid plans because we live in a broken world. We're surrounded by broken people. But we won't be alone. And we aren't without help.

If the Lord is our fortress, it means we are covered on all sides. We're fully surrounded by His love and protection. And if God is our refuge, we have a safe place in the storm. So when you're treated badly, run to Him. God will be with you, working all things for good.

The Lord Is Your Helper

This is why we can confidently say,
The Lord is my helper, and I won't be
afraid. What can people do to me?
HEBREWS 13:6 CEB

. . . .

Betrayal knocks us to our knees. In our confusion, it brings forth fearful thoughts that slowly pick away at our peace. We look at the future, terrified of how we will move forward when all we see is horrible outcomes and endings. And rather than stand strong in faith and lean on God for direction, we crumble.

Be bold, friend. You are tightly held by the Father. And you can be confident things will be okay because God is with you, ready to help. Every broken piece of your life will be restored to something beautiful. He won't let you fall. Your life isn't ruined. So have faith and hope. You're safe with the Lord.

84

Finding Peace in the Stress

Now may the Lord of peace Himself grant you His peace at all times and in every way [that peace and spiritual well-being that comes to those who walk with Him, regardless of life's circumstances]. The Lord be with you all.

2 THESSALONIANS 3:16 AMP

Is your job stressful right now? Maybe there are big projects and tight deadlines ahead. Maybe there's grumbling in the ranks. Maybe the new boss is difficult or the company has been sold. Or maybe there are rumors of layoffs coming. Regardless of the why, the truth is that work isn't a happy place these days.

What a relief to know you can have God's peace "at all times and in every way." No matter your circumstances, He will settle your spirit. And God will bless you with the ability to be content in the most frustrating times.

A Step Back

*There are six things that the LORD hates, seven
things detestable to him: snobbish eyes, a
lying tongue, hands that spill innocent blood, a
heart set on wicked plans, feet that run quickly
to evil, a false witness who breathes lies, and
one who causes conflicts among relatives.*

PROVERBS 6:16–19 CEB

. . . .

Many have been caught in the middle of arguments within
the church. When we're involved, the "curtain" is pulled
back and we can see the inner workings. And often, it's a
huge put-off. We weren't privy to the deeper issues while
sitting in the pews.

Unless you feel specifically called to bring peace, take
a step back. Like disharmony in other situations, church
discord can be a minefield of ways to trap you in sin. And
if you're not an integral part of the healing process, you
don't want to be part of the problem.

86

Coming alongside Others

*All praises belong to the God and Father of
our Lord Jesus Christ. For he is the Father
of tender mercy and the God of endless
comfort. He always comes alongside us
to comfort us in every suffering so that we
can come alongside those who are in any
painful trial. We can bring them this same
comfort that God has poured out upon us.*

2 CORINTHIANS 1:3-4 TPT

What a blessing to read that God *always* comes alongside us with comfort! It's this act of compassion that teaches us how to come alongside others who are suffering too. Knowing someone else has struggled in the same ways brings encouragement, especially when they are full of joy and peace.

Ask God to open your eyes to others who could use your firsthand understanding and support. Be ready to bring comfort just like the Lord did for you.

It's about Where You Focus

Celebrate God all day, every day. I mean, revel in
him! Make it as clear as you can to all you meet
that you're on their side, working with them and
not against them. Help them see that the Master
is about to arrive. He could show up any minute!
PHILIPPIANS 4:4-5 MSG

• •

How would life be more satisfying and less stressful if you spent your days celebrating God's goodness rather than focusing on family frustrations? That's not to mean you hide your head in the sand, refusing to address issues. It just means you keep an eternal perspective. It means you make sure your family knows you're on their side and love them. And it encourages those you care for to not major on the minors.

Instead, choose to live in peace. Keep your home in order and focused on His return over everything else.

Transforming Anger with Peace

*Take care with the things you say. Don't lie or
spread gossip or talk about improper things.
Walk away from the evil things of the world,
and always seek peace and pursue it.*
PSALM 34:13-14 VOICE

. . . .

In your anger, don't sin. That's a tall order, right? But if our
goal is for our words and actions to glorify the Lord, then
how we live matters. We have to think before we speak from
a place of frustration. Our words must be true, kind, and
holy. And when faced with ungodly opportunities, walking
away steers us from chaos, which often breeds irritation.

One of the best ways we can curb our anger is to seek
peace with fervor. We must guard our heart from anything
that threatens to steal it. So choose the path of peace
every time, and watch how it transforms the anger you
often struggle with.

Your Weakness Isn't a Liability

He said to me, "My grace is enough for you, because power is made perfect in weakness." So I'll gladly spend my time bragging about my weaknesses so that Christ's power can rest on me.

2 CORINTHIANS 12:9 CEB

• •

When we feel we've fallen short, remember God's grace makes up the difference. Sometimes we make wrong choices that lead to difficulties like foreclosure. Maybe we worked hard but lost a job anyway. Or maybe life threw us a curveball, and we found ourselves in dire straits. The *how* doesn't matter, because our weakness isn't a liability. Instead, it's the perfect opportunity for God to display His strength and grace.

Do not beat yourself up, friend. We certainly don't live in a perfect world. Instead, have bold faith that God is on the move in your circumstances. Let His power rest on you!

The Dead-End Path

Loving money is a root of all evils. Some people run after it so much that they have given up their faith. Craving more money pushes them away from the faith into error, compounding misery in their lives!

1 TIMOTHY 6:10 TPT

• •

Money itself isn't the root of all evil. It's the *love* of it that gets us into trouble. Why? Because it becomes our god. Rather than be content with what we have, we always want more. We crave bigger and better. And we buy into the world's value system, looking at our success through its lens.

But friend, the path of greed leads to a dead end. We will never find deep contentment there. It's a short-lived scenario that'll leave us wanting more. God is the only one who can fully satisfy. And every time we invest in our relationship with Him, our heart will be filled to overflowing.

The Cascade of Blessings

*But that's not all! Even in times of trouble we
have a joyful confidence, knowing that our
pressures will develop in us patient endurance.
And patient endurance will refine our character,
and proven character leads us back to hope.*

ROMANS 5:3-5 TPT

. . . .

Let it encourage your heart to know the struggles you're
facing with chronic illness don't have to steal your hope
for a beautiful future. That doesn't take away from
the emotional and physical challenges you must face daily.
No one would argue life is easy. But it does allow you to
see that God brings good things from hard things. Your
suffering is not for naught, friend.

Be sure your heart stays free from bitterness and is
instead focused on trusting the Lord's goodness. Doing
so allows the powerful cascade of blessings mentioned in
today's verses to come about. Hold out for hope!

Trusting God with Infertility

Give God the right to direct your life,
and as you trust him along the way,
you'll find he pulled it off perfectly!
PSALM 37:5 TPT

. . . .

If you are struggling with infertility today, be assured that God sees every tear you cry. He understands the complexity of emotions you're feeling. He knows the deep longing of your heart and the pain you experience as each month passes unsuccessfully. And God's desire is for you to trust Him fully because He's on the move.

Surrender your fears to the Lord. Lay your worries and anxieties at His feet. Tell Him you trust His plan for your life. Tell God you believe His timing is always perfect, even when it comes to starting a family. And as you release the expectations you've set, a peace will begin to fill your heart. Good things are ahead!

A New Perspective on Failure

Lord, so many times I fail; I fall into disgrace.
But when I trust in you, I have a strong
and glorious presence protecting and
anointing me. Forever you're all I need!

PSALM 73:26 TPT

. . . .

Failure is just part of life. And while those words are easy to read, the reality of walking them out brings discouragement and dismay. We don't want to fail, because doing so lets others down. It's embarrassing. Even more, it's a powerful reminder we're so far from perfect—something many of us strive for.

But when our trust is in God and not our own strength, it takes the pressure off. We choose to believe in God's will and ways, knowing He'll open doors and close them. It compels us to follow rather than lead. So when something falls flat, we can thank God for guiding us rather than beat ourselves up for failing.

When You're the Cause

*Fathers, do not provoke or irritate or exasperate
your children [with demands that are trivial
or unreasonable or humiliating or abusive;
nor by favoritism or indifference; treat them
tenderly with lovingkindness], so they will
not lose heart and become discouraged or
unmotivated [with their spirits broken].*

COLOSSIANS 3:21 AMP

As parents, are we the cause of stress in the family? Sometimes our best-laid plans in parenting fall short. What we mean for good doesn't translate that way to those we love. And rather than be awesome as we planned them to be, our actions end up being more awful.

We want to raise godly men and women! But make sure expectations are realistic so they don't lose heart or give up. With each step, let God guide your parenting decisions. Ask Him to give you confident and creative ways to grow them to be productive, faith-filled people.

95

God's Calming Presence

*So don't be afraid. I am here, with you;
don't be dismayed, for I am your God. I will
strengthen you, help you. I am here with My
right hand to make right and to hold you up.*
ISAIAH 41:10 VOICE

. . . .

God's presence is so powerful it's able to calm every fear.
It stills our anxious heart better than anything else. Just
realizing God is with us serves as a fail-safe worry buster
because there's no other presence that has command over
what stirs us up. As believers, we must embrace this truth,
acknowledging He's with us in those messy moments.

So when worry starts, pray. Go right to God and tell
Him what you're battling. Ask Him for what you need. Let
Him calm your racing heart and stop you from spiraling
emotionally. You can overcome fear with your faith by
asking for God's help right then, right there.

His Name Is Enough

The name of the LORD is a strong tower;
the righteous runs to it and is safe
and set on high [far above evil].
PROVERBS 18:10 AMP

Sometimes when deep disappointments come our way, all we can do is say the name of Jesus over and over again. We can't find the words to pray because we don't understand the complexity of our emotions. We don't have the mind to form sentences because we've been blindsided by distress. But we can cry out the powerful name of Jesus.

Friend, His name is enough. Scripture says the *name* of the Lord is a strong tower. When it's all you can muster the energy to pray, it is enough. He already knows every detail of your situation. So as believers, it should be our immediate response to hardship. It's how we find safety when our life unexpectedly explodes.

Living Honestly

*Food gained by deceit is sweet to a man,
but afterward his mouth will be filled with
gravel [just as sin may be sweet at first,
but later its consequences bring despair].*

PROVERBS 20:17 AMP

. . . .

For many of us, there's a battle always raging in our heart to live each day with a spirit of honesty. We find ways to justify our fraudulent behavior, usually because it makes our life easier. So when at a crossroads, we're faced with a decision to tell the truth no matter what or mislead to make a situation less complicated.

Lying is often a default button. But for the believer, it should rub us the wrong way. We should feel a catch in our spirit. And while dishonesty may work in the moment, there will be ugly consequences that follow. Choose today to live sincerely and truthfully. . .and you will be blessed!

Honoring Elderly Parents

*"Honor (respect, obey, care for) your father
and your mother, as the LORD your God
has commanded you, so that your days
[on the earth] may be prolonged and so
that it may go well with you in the land
which the LORD your God gives you."*

DEUTERONOMY 5:16 AMP

If we were to be honest, there's often frustration associated with navigating a relationship with our elderly parents. They can become more set in their ways. They may require constant care that's exhausting. And there may be a decline mentally, which is a challenge to deal with regularly. Ask God for the supernatural ability to love and honor your parents in ways that bless them and glorify Him.

And as a bonus, when you care for them with compassion, God promises to bless you too. Your prayerful desire to love them well won't go unnoticed by the Lord.

When You Discover the Affair

*For the Eternal watches over the
righteous, and His ears are attuned to
their prayers. He is always listening.*
PSALM 34:15 VOICE

. . . .

Discovering the secret life of our husband is an unwelcome
and massive shock to the system. And learning of his
affair(s) can literally knock the breath out of us. We're left
with endless questions and fear of the future, and we're
unsure about what to do next. It's absolutely debilitating
on every level.

This is where your faith takes over as every cry becomes
a prayer to the Father. Each groan is carried to His ears,
and God understands their meaning. Our tears become
liquid prayers, and He can read them. When you cling to
the Lord, your grip reveals your pain. God feels it. He is
always listening. So let Him be the one you trust to put
you back together. . .better and stronger.

Why Intoxication Is a Problem

Wine is a mocker, strong drink a riotous brawler;
and whoever is intoxicated by it is not wise.
PROVERBS 20:1 AMP

. . . .

There's no way around it. God's Word is clear about not becoming drunk with alcohol. And while many enjoy it in moderation, when it becomes something we abuse, it isn't in God's will for us. Maybe it's because we lose morality when under the influence. Maybe it's because we use it to escape our issues and challenges. Or maybe it's because alcohol becomes an idol, and God is a jealous God. Regardless, being intoxicated—for whatever reason—is a sin.

To live righteously, be responsible with drinking. If you're abusing it, find the courage to stop. If you need professional help and support, get it. Our life's purpose is to bring glory to God through our words and actions. And when we get drunk, neither of those happens.

The Yucky Feeling of Weakness

After all, it is I, the Eternal One your God, who
has hold of your right hand, who whispers in
your ear, "Don't be afraid. I will help you."
ISAIAH 41:13 VOICE

. . . .

Few things are more demoralizing than when we feel weak, especially when we're used to being effective and capable. At times it seems we're superhuman. From thriving in a career to raising a family to running a home, our "normal" is being an accomplished woman, so to feel anything less is frightening.

Friend, deep breath. Your weakness doesn't intimidate God. He's not disappointed. Instead, He wants you to know He's got you. God is holding your hand through this season, and He's sending a constant reminder to give your fear to Him. Ask the Lord to rework the expectations you've set for yourself, allowing for ups and downs without beating yourself up.

Choosing to Be an Inspiration

*Let us consider how to inspire each other
to greater love and to righteous deeds, not
forgetting to gather as a community, as some
have forgotten, but encouraging each other,
especially as the day of His return approaches.*
HEBREWS 10:24–25 VOICE

When your church members are battling one another for whatever reason, choose to inspire instead of taking sides. Ask God for ways to help bring healing to the community. Where can you be an encourager? How can you foster productivity and kindness at each gathering? How can you bring the love of God into the mix effectively?

While you may not be called to fix the situation, you can pray for healing. You can be a strong advocate for reconciliation. You can be a voice of reason. You can keep an unoffended heart. Let God guide your steps as you listen for His prompting.

None in Heaven

God will wipe away every tear from their eyes; and death shall be no more, neither shall there be anguish (sorrow and mourning) nor grief nor pain any more, for the old conditions and the former order of things have passed away.

REVELATION 21:4 AMPC

. . . .

Every discomfort and all suffering we experience while on earth will disappear when we see Jesus face-to-face. We may be riddled with chronic pain here, but heaven will be free from it. There may be countless doctor visits and treatments now, but we won't need them in eternity.

The "old conditions"—the agony and aching—will be a human experience only. But once we walk through the pearly gates, we'll be able to skip and jump down streets of gold without any pain. Take heart, friend! You will be healed, if not here on earth then once in heaven.

Help When You Feel Helpless

*For Jesus is not some high priest who
has no sympathy for our weaknesses
and flaws. He has already been tested
in every way that we are tested; but He
emerged victorious, without failing God.*

Hebrews 4:15 voice

. . . .

What a gift to know Jesus gets it. When we pray for help, we're praying to the one who has already been tested in every way we are being tested. Nothing is new to Him. The Lord isn't stumped by our circumstances. He isn't dumbfounded by new temptations. Instead, Jesus fully understands the ins and outs of what we're battling.

Knowing that, let Him be your support! Look for Christ's help to get through the helpless feelings. You don't have to figure it out alone, nor do you need to depend on others to bail you out. With Jesus' help, you can emerge victorious, pleasing God with your bold faith.

The Sweet Spot

*You become my delicious feast even when my
enemies dare to fight. You anoint me with the
fragrance of your Holy Spirit; you give me all
I can drink of you until my cup overflows.*

PSALM 23:5 TPT

. . . .

Let your relationship with God be the sweet spot in life,
especially when earthly relationships bring bitterness.
He's genuine and trustworthy, something you may not
experience with others. Time spent with God only brings
good things to life—more strength, keen wisdom, extra joy,
perfect peace, and lasting comfort. It never takes away. It
never places unrealistic or unwanted expectations in our
day. And it gives us a positive perspective, knowing God
is always for us.

Dysfunctional relationships drain us in every way, but
time with God never will. Learn to prioritize your bond
with the Lord over anyone else. He will teach you what a
healthy and functioning relationship looks like.

An Escape Route

We all experience times of testing, which is
normal for every human being. But God will
be faithful to you. He will screen and filter the
severity, nature, and timing of every test or trial
you face so that you can bear it. And each test is
an opportunity to trust him more, for along with
every trial God has provided for you a way of
escape that will bring you out of it victoriously.

1 CORINTHIANS 10:13 TPT

God will be faithful to you, friend! If your desire is to break the addiction cycle and be free of drug abuse—be it prescription or street drugs—God promises you something very important: an escape route.

Even more, scripture says He will "screen and filter" the details of each trial to make sure you can withstand it. And as you trust Him through the fire, you'll find victory from it.

The Field Trippers

*And let us not lose heart and grow weary
and faint in acting nobly and doing right,
for in due time and at the appointed
season we shall reap, if we do not loosen
and relax our courage and faint.*

GALATIANS 6:9 AMPC

. . . .

Some kids are rule followers. They're pleasers who enjoy the straight and narrow. They learn by the textbook of life, making wise choices so they don't get into hard situations.

But then there are the kids who take the field trip. They are the ones who must experience life to learn about it. They don't heed our advice because they need to walk it out themselves. And they sometimes break our heart as we watch them choose unwisely. Mom, don't grow weary or faint in your hopes and prayers. Don't give up in this difficult season. God will honor your persistence.

108

God Is the Hero in Your Story

Hard times may well be the plight of the righteous—they may often seem overwhelmed— but the Eternal rescues the righteous from what oppresses them. He will protect all of their bones; not even one bone will be broken.

PSALM 34:19-20 VOICE

You don't have to be the hero in your story, because God is. So take off the cape and pack it away for good. When you anchor your faith in God and decide He is your rescuer, your superhero garb isn't necessary anymore. In your feelings of helplessness, the Lord is the one to swoop in and save you.

Let God be the strong one so you don't have to. Your job is to trust Him. The only shield you're to hold is the one of faith. And let God—who loves you unwaveringly—take care of the rest.

Taking On Challenges

You see, God did not give us a cowardly spirit
but a powerful, loving, and disciplined spirit.
2 TIMOTHY 1:7 VOICE

· ·

It's because God has given you the spirit of power that you're able to face every challenge that comes your way. It's the courage He instilled in you that allows you to stand strong through trials and tribulations. There is self-control baked in that enables you to focus and make good choices. It's all because of God.

So don't partner with lies saying you're not up for the task at hand. As a believer, you have the Lord's promises to bank on. When you ask, God will give you what you need in the moment. Where you lack, He will fill in the gaps with His goodness. He'll make up the difference with His divinity so you can take on every challenge confidently.

Is It a Solo Mission?

*People do their best making plans for their
lives, but the Eternal guides each step.*
PROVERBS 16:9 VOICE

• •

Sometimes our disappointments come directly from our own pridefulness. Even as believers who understand God to be our good and faithful shepherd, we go ahead and draft plans for our life. It's a solo mission. We get all creative as we set goals, excited for the expected results to rise to the surface. We nerd out as we get organized for the adventure ahead. And we don't even think to ask God what His plans are for our life.

One of the best ways to avoid disappointing situations is to follow God's will rather than get ahead of Him. Before you put in all the time, ask the Lord for insight. Ask for direction. Let Him give you the next right step, and then watch how He blesses your obedient pursuit.

III

Not a Liability

GOD said, "And who do you think made the human mouth? And who makes some mute, some deaf, some sighted, some blind? Isn't it I, GOD? So, get going. I'll be right there with you—with your mouth! I'll be right there to teach you what to say."

EXODUS 4:11-12 MSG

. . . .

Moses argued with God, saying his stutter should exclude him from commanding Pharaoh to let the Israelites go. Sometimes we also believe our disability disqualifies us from serving God in meaningful ways. Rather than put ourselves out there, we stay hidden. And even though we are talented and interested, we're unwilling to risk any kind of rejection. The last thing we want is to feel embarrassment.

Friend, your disability isn't a liability. In fact, it may be what opens the heart of someone who is shy because of their own disability and leads them to embrace Jesus.

Settling Your Nerves

So why would I fear the future? Only goodness and tender love pursue me all the days of my life. Then afterward, when my life is through, I'll return to your glorious presence to be forever with you!
PSALM 23:6 TPT

Surgery can be scary business because we face many unknowns. We may have high hopes, but there's often a twinge of fear in the background. We're literally at the mercy of another, which can feel terribly vulnerable. But God is with you, overseeing the surgery in its entirety.

Keep in mind He has already numbered your days. Before you took your first breath, your life's end had already been determined. And that day is nonnegotiable. At the right time, the Lord will welcome you into heaven. Until then, let your faith in God's goodness and love settle your nerves as you trust His perfect plan.

113

Ask for More Faith

*At once the father of the boy gave
[an eager, piercing, inarticulate] cry
with tears, and he said, Lord, I believe!
[Constantly] help my weakness of faith!*

MARK 9:24 AMPC

. . . .

Many of us can relate to the father in today's verse. Like him, we believe God is all-powerful. We know He is almighty. Chances are we've seen Him move mountains in our life or in the life of someone we love. We believe He is faithful. But in this moment, we're still struggling to trust Him to work wonders in our circumstance. And the struggle is a lack of faith that only God can remedy.

Don't let doubt prevail! Instead, cry out to the Lord for a greater measure of faith. Admit where you're uncertain. Be honest about the hesitation in your spirit. Let God know of your reservation and skepticism. And then ask for a more confident faith.

When You Brought About the Injustice

The Lord redeems the lives of His servants, and none of those who take refuge and trust in Him shall be condemned or held guilty.

PSALM 34:22 AMPC

· ·

Maybe you're the one who wronged someone else. Maybe it was your action that brought hardship to another. Maybe your choices deeply wounded someone you love, and the relationship is now in turmoil. And because of that, you can't help but sit in shame and guilt, unable to move forward. You can't forgive yourself for bringing suffering in such a way.

Let today's verse bring hope to your weary spirit. If you'll allow it, your repentance will usher in redemption. And as you find your refuge in God and trust Him to make right what you've made wrong, a weight will lift off your chest. Any condemnation will evaporate. And God will make you whole again.

Are You to Restore the Dishonest?

*Brothers and sisters, if a person is caught
doing something wrong, you who are spiritual
should restore someone like this with a spirit
of gentleness. Watch out for yourselves so
you won't be tempted too. Carry each other's
burdens and so you will fulfill the law of Christ.*
GALATIANS 6:1-2 CEB

So often, we want to run in the other direction from someone we deem dishonest. We want to slam the door shut on any sort of relationship because trust has been broken. But is that God's desire? You'll need to pray for discernment as you consider the role you're to play.

Friend, maybe God wants you to help restore the corrupt. Maybe you're to come alongside the fraudulent as they repent and ask God to restore. Maybe He will use you to bring a change of heart to the deceitful. Ask Him for clarity.

God's Presence Is with You

*This is My command: be strong and
courageous. Never be afraid or discouraged
because I am your God, the Eternal One, and
I will remain with you wherever you go.*

JOSHUA 1:9 VOICE

. . . .

Litigation can be lengthy, costly, and emotionally draining.
And it can be terrifying. Your best defense as you walk
this out is to take God with you every time you enter the
mediation room or courtroom. Listen for His wisdom and
discernment for your next steps. Ask God to replace your
anxious heart with bold courage, and let Him create in
you a confidence to stand up for yourself.

God is with you wherever you go. From the moment you
wake till your head hits the pillow at night, His presence
will be your safe place. And it will also be what gives you
the strength to stand strong.

Worry Adds Nothing

*"Does worry add anything to your life?
Can it add one more year, or even one
day? So if worrying adds nothing, but
actually subtracts from your life, why would
you worry about God's care of you?"*

LUKE 12:25-26 TPT

. . . .

If worry helped us one bit, then it would be worth the energy expended. But worry does nothing to help remedy our circumstances. It doesn't calm our nerves or end our fearful thoughts. When we worry, the stress doesn't go away. And we don't experience peace or joy when we focus on all that could go wrong. Worry adds nothing but heartache to our life.

Jesus came to give you freedom, and worry removes it. We become enslaved to what burdens us. So ask God to help you learn to trust Him over focusing your time and energy on what you have no control over.

The Pit of Depression

I've learned that his anger lasts for a moment,
but his loving favor lasts a lifetime! We may
weep through the night, but at daybreak
it will turn into shouts of ecstatic joy.

PSALM 30:5 TPT

• •

When you mess up, don't beat yourself up. Doing so doesn't change how things turned out. It doesn't fix anything. And it doesn't reflect how God feels about your choices. But it does give you a one-way ticket to the pit of depression. As a believer, that's not the residence God has for you.

Sometimes depression is situational and other times clinical. Take time to learn more about how you're feeling and why. But know God didn't create you for self-hate. You weren't made to live in chronic unhappiness. Spend time with Him, allowing God to reveal root causes. And then ask for guidance on what to do next.

Choose Peace above All Else

Stay away from anger and revenge. Keep envy far from you, for it only leads you into lies. For one day the wicked will be destroyed, but those who trust in the Lord will inherit the land.

PSALM 37:8-9 TPT

Sometimes our anger is righteous, but other times it leads to sinful behavior. Anger makes us lash out, hoping to hurt the one who hurt us. It encourages vengeful thoughts and plans in hopes of satisfying our deep frustration. And it leaves us bankrupt of love and compassion, something God specifically commands us to show toward others.

It's imperative to get anger under control. We cannot live righteous lives if our temper is what controls us every time something doesn't go our way. If you want God's bountiful blessings, let Him heal your anger. Ask for it. Choose peace above all else, and let God do the rest.

Ministry of Presence

He heals the wounds of every shattered heart.
PSALM 147:3 TPT

. . . .

When you lose a child, there are no sufficient words that will bring any comfort. No platitudes or cute Christian sayings will offer help in any way. Trying to justify someone's loss—even with pure motives—can't bring any good to the situation. And this isn't the time to share silver-lining insight to which we subscribe. We just need to stop trying to fix things and let the grieving. . .grieve.

What we can offer is something called the ministry of presence. It's being with the one grieving without offering solutions for the pain. It's crying with the parent suffering loss. And it's meeting needs like cleaning, cooking, and running errands. God is the only one who can heal their shattered heart. We're to be His hands and feet while He does.

Have Nothing to Do with Greed

*As the saying goes: Those who love money
will never be satisfied with money, and
those who love riches will never be happy
with what they have. This, too, is fleeting.*
ECCLESIASTES 5:10 VOICE

• •

Every day you have a choice. Will you embrace what is fleeting or will you anchor yourself to truth? Will you choose to follow a worldly narrative or cling to God's Word? Friend, will you chase after fame and fortune or follow passionately after the Lord? You can't do both, so a choice must be made.

Greed is dangerous for the heart of a believer because it takes the focus off God and becomes selfish in nature. It creates new gods to worship with our time and effort. And it will do nothing but cultivate discontentment and rob you of peace. Have nothing to do with it.

Continual Renewal

*And don't go on lying to each other since you
have sloughed away your old skin along with
its evil practices for a fresh new you, which is
continually renewed in knowledge according
to the image of the One who created you.*
COLOSSIANS 3:9–10 VOICE

· ·

Just take it day by day. When you're trying to live a life
pleasing to God, understand that old habits will try to
entangle you. The enemy doesn't want you to be free
from his grip and will do all he can to entice you into old
behaviors.

But God promises to continually renew you in knowledge. As you spend time in prayer and in the Word, you
will learn about the Lord and His will. Your heart will be
transformed, and you will have the strength through faith
to live an honest and honoring life that blesses you and
glorifies God.

Seeking God's Guidance

*Trust in the Lord completely, and do not rely
on your own opinions. With all your heart
rely on him to guide you, and he will lead
you in every decision you make. Become
intimate with him in whatever you do,
and he will lead you wherever you go.*

PROVERBS 3:5-6 TPT

When facing sickness, ask God for guidance on what to do next. We're often too emotionally involved to know what's best, but your Father knows. Scripture says to trust Him completely, not your own opinions. So let God speak into your situation and provide a path for you to follow.

Are you wondering which treatment option is best? Are you weighing the pros and cons of surgery? Are you confused by a diagnosis and feel unsettled by the doctor's suggestions? Rely on God's guidance. The more time you spend in His presence, the clearer His answers will become.

But You Can Trust God's Word

Every scripture is inspired by God and is useful for teaching, for showing mistakes, for correcting, and for training character, so that the person who belongs to God can be equipped to do everything that is good.

2 TIMOTHY 3:16–17 CEB

If you struggle trusting others to be honest and candid, rest in God's Word. It's a truth teller. Through its pages, it will effectively shed light on any plan you've concocted to ensure integrity. If you're wondering how to best handle a tough situation, it will teach and train. Scripture will convict your actions and equip you for what's ahead.

Even more, the Bible isn't full of half truths. Every word is God-inspired, which is why you can trust the truths in its pages over the advice of anyone else. If you're a skeptic by nature, let His Word guide you through life.

Remember

*Blessed be GOD, my mountain, who trains
me to fight fair and well. He's the bedrock on
which I stand, the castle in which I live, my
rescuing knight, the high crag where I run
for dear life, while he lays my enemies low.*

PSALM 144:1-2 MSG

. . . .

When you get the dreaded phone call with news of
an accident, let your faith rise up. These are moments
we need reminders of who God is and what He can do.
We need to know of His protection and compassion,
and we need these truths in our heart so we can access
them immediately.

Remember that God is your foundation, enabling
you to stand. He's the castle that surrounds you and the
knight who rescues. God is the mountain you run to for
help because He's faithful. Let Him steady your heart
with reminders of His awesomeness as you navigate the
difficult road ahead.

Avoid Rotten Fruit

All the things the world can offer to you—the allure of pleasure, the passion to have things, and the pompous sense of superiority—do not come from the Father. These are the rotten fruits of this world. This corrupt world is already wasting away, as are its selfish desires. But the person really doing God's will—that person will never cease to be.

1 JOHN 2:16-17 VOICE

. . . .

Choose the good fruit of the Spirit and not the rotten fruits of the world, for they lead to corruption. Our earthly wants create an insatiable desire that's hard to fill—an addiction to what makes us feel good. We're satisfied only for a moment, and then we crave more.

But focusing our yearnings on the pursuit of righteous living creates a contentment that removes our need for the rotten fruit of earthly addictions. Everything here becomes strangely dim in the light of eternity.

Comparison

If anyone thinks they are important when they aren't, they're fooling themselves. Each person should test their own work and be happy with doing a good job and not compare themselves with others. Each person will have to carry their own load.

GALATIANS 6:3-5 CEB

. . . .

It's been said that comparison is the thief of joy. It robs you of seeing the beautiful creation you are. And this dysfunctional mindset is a sure way to ruin a friendship.

Whether you see yourself as better than or less than someone else, it's incorrect. There's no way to effectively compare because you were made special and unique on purpose. They were too. Why not celebrate the differences and cheer each other on? When it's hard, ask God to help you! Let Him give you confidence so you're not reckless in relationships. He will empower you to be compassionate and caring, creating healthy friendships that last.

Being a Comfort for Others

*He's the one who comforts us in all our trouble
so that we can comfort other people who are
in every kind of trouble. We offer the same
comfort that we ourselves received from God.*

2 CORINTHIANS 1:4 CEB

If you've lost a spouse, you're the perfect person to support others who have suffered the same kind of loss. You bring a unique perspective and a full understanding not everyone has. You've walked this difficult path and have made it safely to the other side. Consider that God wants to use your hard-won wisdom to be an encouragement to someone else.

Are you open to it? Why not let your church know your willingness to help? Are there local support groups to join? Be on the lookout for opportunities to be a source of comfort for the heartbroken. They could use some sweet reassurance.

Confident Faith

Just make sure you ask empowered by confident faith without doubting that you will receive. For the ambivalent person believes one minute and doubts the next. Being undecided makes you become like the rough seas driven and tossed by the wind. You're up one minute and tossed down the next.

JAMES 1:6 TPT

· ·

There's a big difference between asking God for something and asking Him with confident faith. Maybe you've seen this contrast when your child asked for a raise in allowance. Or when an employee asked for additional time off. Maybe it was visible when they asked you to be the volunteer chairperson. And chances are you responded favorably when you saw their boldness. You appreciated their assuredness in your kindness.

Your confidence isn't arrogant or demanding. It's asking God with full faith, knowing He is with you and for you. It's trusting He'll make good on every promise made.

God's Door

GOD's a safe-house for the battered, a sanctuary
during bad times. The moment you arrive,
you relax; you're never sorry you knocked.
PSALM 9:9–10 MSG

. . . .

When battling depression, so often we just want a safe house—a place of protection from the wiles of the world. We want to tuck away with God in His sanctuary and be comforted. And we want it fast. Be it from fear, insecurity, trauma, heartache, or fatigue from our circumstances, there is no margin left in our heart.

Friend, don't you know God is ready right now? He's waiting for you to come into His presence and be reassured. In those moments when you're overwhelmed by a sense of sadness and hopelessness, His door is open. Let it be your first knock—your immediate response to a depressive situation. Scripture says you won't be sorry you did.

131

When They Walk Away from the Faith

I also know how you have bravely endured trials and persecutions because of my name, yet you have not become discouraged.
REVELATION 2:3 TPT

These words were written to the church at Ephesus at God's command. While John affirmed them in the letter, he later tells them they've lost their first love. The directive was to turn back to God and once again respond in the faithful ways they had in the past.

Let this be your prayer as you fight on your knees for a child who's walked away from their faith. As a Christian mom, your prayers have weight when it comes to your kids, and praying scripture adds to it. So ask God to stir their heart so they return to Him in faith. Ask Him to restore the heart of your child so they have desire and motivation to find their way back.

God-Loving Counsel

God-lovers make the best counselors.
Their words possess wisdom and are right
and trustworthy. The ways of God are in
their hearts and they won't swerve from
the paths of steadfast righteousness.

PSALM 37:30–31 TPT

• •

If you're struggling and in need of counsel, make sure to choose wisely. Be it a close friend, a parent, or a licensed professional, it's important they are believers. There may be wonderful people who love you and have hard-won wisdom, but unless they understand the vital role God plays in your life, their advice may not be doctrinally sound. Even with every good intention, they just don't have the same foundation you have.

But when they are God lovers, His words will flow through them and into your weary heart. They will help you navigate the difficult arguments and painful heartaches you're having to face right now.

133

Strength for Leaving

*I look up to the mountains; does my
strength come from mountains? No, my
strength comes from GOD, who made
heaven, and earth, and mountains.*

PSALM 121:1–2 MSG

. . . .

If you're experiencing violence in any way, it's time for
you to walk away and seek help. Yes, this is a complex
situation with many issues to consider. Of course it feels
scary to make a decision of this magnitude. And you may
not feel strong enough to walk this out in real time. But
God will strengthen you for the moment.

Don't depend on your humanity to make this happen,
because we are weak and unable to take such giant steps at
times. We simply don't have what it takes. But God knows
this and has made provision, promising to give you the
strength necessary to protect yourself by choosing to leave.

Shame in Divorce and Separation

Don't be afraid, for there is no one to shame you. Don't fear humiliation, for there is no one to disgrace you. The shame of your younger years and the sorrow of your widowhood are over. You'll forget those days as if they never happened.

ISAIAH 54:4 VOICE

• •

Many of us also feel a sense of shame because our marriage failed. Shame is real and devastating. Because of it, when we separate or divorce, we often decide there's something wrong with who we are as a woman. And it leads us into questioning our goodness. We feel unlovable because someone stopped loving us.

Shame has knots that tangle your heart. This is where you dig in with your faith and choose to believe Him. Don't let those worthless messages creep in. At the first sign of them, go right to God, and He'll remind you of your value.

Making a Way for You

*Faith opened the way for the Hebrews to
cross the Red Sea as if on dry land, but
when the Egyptians tried to cross they
were swallowed up and drowned!*
HEBREWS 11:29 TPT

If God can part a sea, enabling the Israelites to cross on dry ground and escape the Egyptian army, He can also make a way for your heart to heal. Nothing is impossible with Him. It may feel impossible, but God is fully and completely capable.

Losing a child is the worst kind of pain that makes your heart feel as if it's going to shatter into a million pieces. It's unimaginable. Friend, only God can heal this in you. Don't waste another moment without Him. Like He did for the Israelites, trust the Lord to part the sea of heartache and make a way for you too.

When Anxiety Is a Constant Companion

"I repeat: Don't let worry enter your life. Live above the anxious cares about your personal needs. People everywhere seem to worry about making a living, but your heavenly Father knows your every need and will take care of you."

LUKE 12:29–30 TPT

· ·

In a world of uncertainty, many of us would admit that anxiety is a constant companion that ruins our day. There are a million things to worry about. From relational struggles to health concerns to financial stressors, it takes great faith to release them into God's hands.

Scripture says we shouldn't even let worry invade the nooks and crannies of our life. Instead, we should live above worry. How do we do that? We choose to trust that God knows our needs and will make sure they are met. In prayer, we faithfully unpack each anxious thought and let God figure it out.

It's Not Your Responsibility

You're going to find that there will be times when people will have no stomach for solid teaching, but will fill up on spiritual junk food—catchy opinions that tickle their fancy. They'll turn their backs on truth and chase mirages. But you—keep your eye on what you're doing; accept the hard times along with the good; keep the Message alive; do a thorough job as God's servant.

2 TIMOTHY 4:3–5 MSG

• •

Be careful when you get in heated debates about faith with those at a different level of maturity. You may be a meat-and-potatoes kind of believer and they may feast on spiritual junk food, but peace is possible and should be pursued.

Everyone grows at different times and in a variety of ways, but their relationship with God isn't your responsibility. So pray. Encourage them. And stay focused on your own faith journey.

He Understands What You're Facing

*Friends, when life gets really difficult,
don't jump to the conclusion that God
isn't on the job. Instead, be glad that
you are in the very thick of what Christ
experienced. This is a spiritual refining
process, with glory just around the corner.*
1 PETER 4:12–13 MSG

Let it bring relief that, as you pray to the Lord about your own dying experience, you're praying to the one who faced death Himself. Be comforted in knowing you're not alone. God the Son has a firsthand understanding and will journey through it with you.

Ask Him to direct you to scripture that will help prepare your heart. Ask the Lord to give you confidence, knowing your last breath here will lead to your first breath in heaven. Ask Him for the grace to walk this path full of faith and expectation for eternity.

When You Don't Feel Good Enough

*The fear of man brings a snare, but whoever
leans on, trusts in, and puts his confidence
in the Lord is safe and set on high.*

PROVERBS 29:25 AMPC

For many of us, a big cause of anxiety is feeling like we are not good enough. We feel inadequate as a wife. . .a mom . . .a daughter. . .a friend. . .a coworker. In our desire to be loved, we let others shape how we feel about ourselves. We decide what they think about us is truth, and we forfeit who God says we are, adopting labels from the world.

Said with love and grace, stop it. For too long, we've allowed our value to be diminished by others. God made you! And while you're not perfect, you were made on purpose. Release the anxiety that comes from feeling judged. You are His beloved!

Knowing God Is Guarding You

*GOD guards you from every evil, he guards
your very life. He guards you when you
leave and when you return, he guards
you now, he guards you always.*
PSALM 121:7-8 MSG

As believers, we are protected by God. He guards us daily, promising to be our personal security detail at all times. And for those of us who have trust issues, this is fantastic news.

If you've been hurt in the past, it's hard to have confidence in others. And when it's been a frustrating pattern in life, we become reluctant to put ourselves out there again. But if God promises to be with you always—protecting and restoring—maybe you can step out in faith. Life is full of letdowns we can't avoid, but knowing the Lord will guard us should be all the confidence we need to try again.

Fear of Speaking in Court

"When they take you and turn you over [to the court], do not worry beforehand about what to say, but say whatever is given to you [by God] in that hour; for it is not you who speak, but it is the Holy Spirit [who will speak through you]."

MARK 13:11 AMP

The thought of sitting on the stand in court is unnerving. What you say in that moment carries a lot of weight. It's recorded. It's official. And we get stressed out, worried we'll say the wrong thing or won't have the right words to communicate effectively.

Let today's verse build your confidence that God will give you what you need to say. He will fill your mouth with the words to speak. So let Him calm your heart for the courtroom, knowing the Lord will give you everything necessary to defend yourself with integrity.

Your Faith Delivers You

But the Lord will be the Savior of all who love him. Even in their time of trouble, God will live in them as strength. Because of their faith in him, their daily portion will be a Father's help and deliverance from evil. This is true for all who turn to hide themselves in him!

PSALM 37:39-40 TPT

. . . .

Many of us experience abuse in life. It could be verbal abuse from a parent or spiritual abuse from the church. It may be physical abuse in marriage or a terribly dysfunctional friendship where you suffer emotional abuse. Life can be hard and unfair. But as believers, let's never forget we have the strength of God living in us.

Because of it, we have confidence to walk away. We have courage to report. And we have the energy to call it out. Through your faith, God will bring deliverance.

143

Fear of Bankruptcy

*"But the LORD is the one who is marching
before you! He is the one who will be with
you! He won't let you down. He won't abandon
you. So don't be afraid or scared!"*

DEUTERONOMY 31:8 CEB

. . . .

It's difficult not to be afraid or scared when we're facing bankruptcy. It can leave us feeling ashamed. We may feel like a failure even if we tried our very best to avoid it. And making such a declaration leaves us worried for what comes next. We're concerned about having our basic needs met, and the stress from it is overwhelming.

When the Bible says God is with you, don't let the weight of that statement pass you by. His presence is everything! Cry out to the Lord, sharing your fears and asking for His help. You're not alone, and God won't let you down.

Wasted Time

You have already wasted enough time living like those outsiders in the society around you: losing yourselves in sex, in addictions and desires, in drinking and lawless idolatry, in giving your time and allegiance to things that are not godly.

1 PETER 4:3 VOICE

. . . .

God made you on purpose and for a purpose. He thought you up and determined a path you are to walk in faith. Yes, there is a beautiful calling in your life—something unique you're to accomplish. And every minute you give to abusing alcohol is one that scripture says is wasted time.

Don't abandon your God-created call for anything this world has to offer. They are cheap substitutes for what God has planned, and they have no redeeming quality. They have no eternal value. So ask God to help you change your focus and forgo earthly addictions and desires.

Grieving the Death of a Parent

*Blessed and enviably happy [with a happiness
produced by the experience of God's
favor and especially conditioned by the
revelation of His matchless grace] are those
who mourn, for they shall be comforted!*

MATTHEW 5:4 AMPC

When you lose a parent, it's hard to imagine you will ever be happy again. In the moment, the grief that accompanies the loss feels too much to handle. Your parent has always been the strong one for you—a rock in troubled times. So to have your parent gone feels destabilizing. Your heart is broken.

God says those who mourn shall be comforted. He will surround you in His love and heal the heartache one day at a time. And the pain will eventually subside and become bearable. Your Father will do this for you because of deep and unwavering compassion for His beloved.

Discerning Truth from Lies

*Make sure no predator makes you his
prey through some misleading philosophy
and empty deception based on traditions
fabricated by mere mortals. These are sourced
in the elementary principles originating
in this world and not in the Anointed One
(so don't let their talks capture you).*
COLOSSIANS 2:8 VOICE

Every day, before your feet hit the floor, ask God to fill you
with wisdom. For in this world of smooth talkers, we'll need
to be able to effectively discern between right and wrong.
We'll need the Holy Spirit to help us determine truth versus
lies. If we choose incorrectly, we may set ourselves up for
an emotionally abusive situation that leads us from God.

His wisdom keeps us on the path of righteousness. We
need divine direction in a world where truth is a moving
target. And for that, God is our only hope.

Heartsick

*The heart is most devious and incurably sick.
Who can understand it? It is I, the Eternal
One, who probes the innermost heart and
examines the innermost thoughts. I will
compensate each person justly, according to
his ways and by what his actions deserve.*

JEREMIAH 17:9–10 VOICE

. . . .

Sometimes our sickness is physical. We have aches and pains. We contract diseases. And we battle chronic symptoms that won't go away. But other times, our sickness is emotional. It's in the depths of our heart. It leads us away from God's will and into sinful thoughts and behaviors. And only the Lord can heal it.

When you are stuck in sin, ask God to heal your heart. It's from the heart that we act out in ungodly ways. So when it's purified and renewed, it will show in the way we live. Our sickly heart will be restored once again.

You Have Access to God's Strength

*If you fall apart during a crisis, then you
weren't very strong to begin with.*
PROVERBS 24:10 VOICE

. . . .

When we aren't anchored in faith and trusting God each day, every crisis that comes our way has the ability to knock us down. Honestly, it doesn't take much to send us over the edge when we're functioning in our own strength. Our foundation is built on sinking sand, especially when we're already feeling weak and discouraged.

Listen up, friend. As a believer, you have full and complete access to God's strength. That means when the curveball comes, you can pray for endurance with expectation. You can ask for wisdom and discernment with confidence. You can request a deeper measure of faith so you can believe His promises. Don't stand in defeat another day, because with God you are victorious!

How Serving Others Restores Hope

Don't burn out; keep yourselves fueled and aflame. Be alert servants of the Master, cheerfully expectant. Don't quit in hard times; pray all the harder. Help needy Christians; be inventive in hospitality.

ROMANS 12:11-13 MSG

. . . .

One of the ways you can battle feelings of hopelessness is to serve others. Often, getting our mind off our own problems helps us gain a new perspective. We stop staring at the circumstances that feel overwhelming to us and instead refocus on helping others. There is something cathartic about meeting the needs of someone else. And in an odd turn of events, we find ourselves blessed for blessing those around us.

Look for opportunities to love others. Spend time with like-minded people who feel compassion for the "least of these." And then watch how your hopeless feelings melt away as you see God's hand moving in miraculous and meaningful ways.

God Sees and Cares

"What's the price of two or three pet canaries? Some loose change, right? But God never overlooks a single one."

LUKE 12:6 MSG

· ·

How comforting to know God sees when we lose a pet. He recognizes how important our furry friends are and understands the sadness we feel when they die. Don't you realize the Lord created them as companions for us? In His sovereignty, God knew the comfort and company they would provide to those He loved.

So take every ounce of grief to Him. Share the depths of your despair in detail. Unlock every bit of sadness and lay it at God's feet. He will help you process the pain. Your tears are safe in His caring hands. And God will make a way for healing, restoring your heart to embrace another pet to love.

You're Not Done For

*And then, after your brief suffering, the
God of all loving grace, who has called you
to share in his eternal glory in Christ, will
personally and powerfully restore you and
make you stronger than ever. Yes, he will
set you firmly in place and build you up.*

1 PETER 5:10 TPT

. . . .

Friend, it's not the end of the road. You're not done for.
You may have lost your job, but that doesn't mean you
have to also lose hope! God tells us suffering is brief and
is followed by restoration and strength. There may be fear
and stress associated with this new development, but God
has you in His capable hands.

So stand strong in faith, asking what comes next. Ask
for guidance. And watch closely for the open doors of
opportunity that will come your way. God is not done with
you, so don't give up on yourself.

Greed Doesn't Look Good on You

He who leans on and trusts in and is confident in his riches will fall, but the righteous [who trust in God's provision] will flourish like a green leaf.
PROVERBS 11:28 AMP

Today's verse is clear about the two places we can anchor our confidence. We can choose to rely on money and wealth, letting it be what calms our anxious heart. We can work for more and more money so we feel secure. We can trust it will always come through, keeping us safe from hardships. Or we can choose to believe God is who He says He is. . .and will do what He says He will do.

The truth is this world wants your allegiance. It wants your attention. And it's doing all it can to create strongholds that pull you off the path of righteousness. Don't let it. Greed never looks good on a believer.

Removed from Pressure Places

When trouble surrounded me, I cried out to the Eternal; He answered me and brought me to a wide, open space. The Eternal is with me, so I will not be afraid of anything. If God is on my side, how can anyone hurt me?

PSALM 118:5-6 VOICE

. . . .

Betrayal hurts because it hits the center of our heart. We've chosen to trust someone with the deepest part of our person. So when we discover the deception, it shatters us. What a blessing to know we have an all-powerful and loving God who saves.

In those times when pain is pressing in on you, cry out to God. He'll remove you from the places of pressure and give you breathing room. You'll be free to stand strong in faith knowing God is on your side, and you'll be unafraid of those who've broken your trust and caused you harm.

Snatched from Dysfunctional Relationships

*I was pushed back, attacked so that I was
about to fall, but the Eternal was there to
help me keep my balance. He is my strength,
and He is the reason I sing; He has been
there to save me in every situation.*

PSALM 118:13-14 VOICE

. . . .

Many times we don't even realize we're in a dysfunctional relationship. Like a frog in a pot of water, we don't recognize each time they turn up the heat. And it's not until things are boiling over that we see the way we've been mistreated all along.

Look to God for balance. When you commit to praying over your relationships, He will reveal sketchy circumstances. He'll help you discern when something feels off. And when it's gone too far, God will snatch you from the situation and save you. Let His love be why you rejoice today!

Family Feuds over Faith

*But Martha became exasperated with finishing
the numerous household chores in preparation
for her guests, so she interrupted Jesus and
said, "Lord, don't you think it's unfair that my
sister left me to do all the work by myself?
You should tell her to get up and help me."*

LUKE 10:40 TPT

Martha chose to be in the kitchen, while Mary wanted to be close to Jesus. Martha decided to bless Him through hospitality, while Mary blessed Him with her undivided heart. Both sisters loved in a different way, and tension ensued because of it.

Family feuds about faith happen. It may be over denomination or church attendance. It may be over doctrine. Or it may be over the existence of God. But if your goal is to love one another well, let that love be what keeps the peace. It may not be the time or environment to hash it out.

Thanking God for Elderly Parents

*You are my God, and I give You thanks; You
are my God, and I praise You. Give thanks
to our Eternal Lord; He is always good.
He never ceases to be loving and kind.*
PSALM 118:28–29 VOICE

. . . .

Give God thanks for your elderly parents. They may require
time you don't have. There may be memory issues to navigate. And they may have become mean and rude in their
old age. But none of that precludes you from praising the
Lord for the role they've played in your life. Taking care
of them, even if inconvenient, both blesses them and
delights God.

God decided your mom and dad were the right fit for
you. In their imperfection, He knew they'd help guide
your path. And He worked through them—even if they
were unaware—getting you to where you are today. That's
worthy of praise, indeed.

Pursuing God above All Else

*"As you passionately seek his kingdom,
above all else, he will supply your needs.
So don't ever be afraid, dearest friends!
Your loving Father joyously gives you
his kingdom with all its promises!"*

LUKE 12:31–32 TPT

. . . .

Put God above all else, and watch as every need you have is met. That means you trust Him over your fear. You seek God over worldly solutions. You pursue Him over the go-tos that take the edge off from time to time. It's challenging, but so worth it.

When we feel lacking in any way, fear naturally comes barreling at us head-on. It exposes a lack of faith. It reveals an unsettled heart that's worried we won't have what we need. And our temptation is to respond with quick fixes and earthly remedies. Friend, you can trust God's promise to care for you. His vow will prevail, guaranteed.

Your Testimony Matters

Moses told Jethro the whole story. He told him everything that the Eternal had done to Pharaoh and the Egyptians on behalf of Israel. He told him about all the misery and tribulations they had run into during their long journey. And then he told how the Eternal had rescued them.

EXODUS 18:8 VOICE

Consider that your testimony helps others find courage in their own situation. In the above verse, Moses shares the struggles and challenges they faced and then reveals how God intervened in meaningful ways. That revelation is what many need to hear. It's the special sauce that keeps them standing strong in faith.

Always be ready to share your story with others. Who knows, but it might be the exact reason others are able to remove doubt and grab on to hope. We all need reminders that God is in the business of miracles.

Connecting through Suffering

*Beloved friends, if life gets extremely difficult,
with many tests, don't be bewildered as though
something strange were overwhelming you.
Instead, continue to rejoice, for you, in a measure,
have shared in the sufferings of the Anointed
One so that you can share in the revelation of his
glory and celebrate with even greater gladness!*

1 PETER 4:12–13 TPT

• •

Scripture tells us to rejoice through the disappointments life brings. Rather than sit in confusion and self-pity when we fail, we're to fix our eyes on the goodness of God. We're to recognize the hardship Jesus faced and let that bring a sense of comradery, understanding the privilege we have to share in suffering.

Failure naturally brings consequences, but falling short is just part of life. And each letdown can be a humble opportunity to connect with the Lord as we experience suffering.

The Rocky Road of Bankruptcy

GOD is good, a hiding place in tough times.
He recognizes and welcomes anyone looking
for help, no matter how desperate the trouble.
NAHUM 1:7 MSG

. . . .

No matter how desperate the trouble you face—like being forced to file for bankruptcy—God is standing with open arms, welcoming you into His protection. Let the Lord be your hiding place and shelter. Let Him be your helper. When you feel overwhelmed by shame manifesting as embarrassment, take it to the Lord. Your heart is safe in His hands.

Let God strengthen you for the road ahead. It may be rocky. But have no fear, for you are loved and valued. And contrary to what the world preaches, you don't have to be perfect. Mistakes and failures are part of the human experience. And always keep in mind that bankruptcy doesn't define you. God does.

A Fresh Start

GOD gives a hand to those down on their luck,
gives a fresh start to those ready to quit.
PSALM 145:14 MSG

. . . .

When a marriage fails, many times we just want to quit at everything. Our motivation to get through the day hits rock bottom. Our desire to take the next step wanes. What we want more than anything is to crawl back into bed and pull the covers over our head. Our heart just isn't in it anymore.

But as believers, we are victorious. There is hope and help waiting for us through God. And while we may want to hide away, it's not what the mighty in faith do. We may get knocked down for a moment, but it doesn't last for long. Need a fresh start? Let God give you the hand up necessary to stand strong and look forward to His goodness to follow.

When Life Piles On

Answer me, LORD—and quickly! My breath is fading. Don't hide your face from me or I'll be like those going down to the pit! Tell me all about your faithful love come morning time, because I trust you. Show me the way I should go, because I offer my life up to you.

PSALM 143:7-8 CEB

Sometimes life piles on. We feel hit from all sides, unable to catch our breath, and we struggle to see any relief. In our overwhelmed state, we can't seem to find hope. We feel panicky because we aren't bouncing back like in the past. Desperation sets in.

If you're there today, ask yourself where God is. Have you taken your troubles to Him, or are you trying to fix things yourself? Trust your life to God, and He will guide you through the muck and mire.

163

Walking through the Grief

*"I've told you all this so that trusting me,
you will be unshakable and assured, deeply
at peace. In this godless world you will
continue to experience difficulties. But
take heart! I've conquered the world."*

JOHN 16:33 MSG

- -

The hard truth is that we *will* experience painful loss, like the death of a beloved spouse. We may try all we can to avoid it, but God's Word is clear. Difficulties are inevitable. And He tells us this for good reason. As we trust Him through our immeasurable grief, God will steady us. We will be assured of His love, and we'll experience a deep peace.

Friend, the only way to get past grief is to walk right through it. You'll experience the deep darkness of the valleys, and God will be there every step of the way. The journey may be long, but you'll be okay. He'll ensure it.

God Is Watching over Your Spouse

*Precious [and of great consequence] in
the sight of the LORD is the death of His
godly ones [so He watches over them].*
PSALM 116:15 AMP

• •

Let it comfort your heart to know God is watching over your spouse even in death. It's your husband's faith while on earth that caused the Lord to consider his death precious. Now they are united in eternity, and it's there God will watch over him. He's safe and sound in the Lord's presence.

Can you just imagine the front-row seat to His glory experienced every day? Go ahead and praise the Lord for the freedom your beloved has from any pain and suffering. Thank Him for the new, glorified body your husband is walking around in. And share your genuine appreciation for God's tender, loving care of him until you arrive in eternity yourself.

Humankind Just Isn't Perfect

We can never look to men for help; no matter who they are, they can't save us, for even our great leaders fail and fall. They too are just mortals who will one day die. At death the spirits of all depart and their bodies return to dust. In the day of their death all their projects and plans are over.

PSALM 146:3-4 TPT

· ·

We want to trust those we love. It's part of what makes a relationship strong, right? When we let others in, it means we are choosing to trust them with our heart. We're exposing our greatest places of wounding, leaving us vulnerable. But humankind isn't perfect and even with best intentions will let us down.

God is the one who's fully faithful. He's always trustworthy. And you can safely place every fear and insecurity in His dependable hands.

Faith and Chronic Pain

Now faith brings our hopes into reality and becomes the foundation needed to acquire the things we long for. It is all the evidence required to prove what is still unseen.

HEBREWS 11:1 TPT

Faith is our firm foundation that makes life worth living. But for many, chronic pain makes life unbearable. So how do these two coexist? While the daily pain you feel is real and difficult, God has made a way for peace and joy. If your foundation is faith, then you choose to trust His plan for your life even if it's hard to understand.

On this side of heaven, we may never be healed. We may battle pain and suffer in terrible ways. But that doesn't have to undo our faith. Done right, it will only strengthen it as we find ourselves relying on Him for hope and help.

When the Battle Is His

*The Lord will fight for you, and you shall
hold your peace and remain at rest.*
EXODUS 14:14 AMPC

. . . .

When you're faced with the deterioration of your marriage, let God be what steadies your heart. He will hold you upright as you navigate the mediation room and court-room. God will direct you to the right counsel. He will protect you in the settlement. He will give you wisdom for details that need to be discussed. Your world may feel like it's crumbling, but God will fight for you. He knows your areas of weakness and will meet them with His strength.

This is a time for the kind of radical faith that leans solely on God for help. There are circumstances where He asks us to fight using the blessing of His provision. And there are other times we're to rest. Both require eyes on God.

Your Body Is a Temple

*Or don't you know that your body is a temple of
the Holy Spirit who is in you? Don't you know that
you have the Holy Spirit from God, and you don't
belong to yourselves? You have been bought
and paid for, so honor God with your body.*

1 CORINTHIANS 6:19–20 CEB

. . . .

Consider that since your body is the temple of the Holy
Spirit, how you treat it matters. God's Spirit is living inside
you. It's a sacred place. And when you choose to abuse
it with drugs, you're denigrating the holy with something
unholy.

Scripture tells us to honor God with our body. Are you
doing that? If not, what needs to change? If you require
help, be quick to ask for it. Always choose righteous living.

Stored Tears

*You've kept track of all my wandering and
my weeping. You've stored my many tears in
your bottle—not one will be lost. For they are
all recorded in your book of remembrance.*

PSALM 56:8 TPT

. . . .

Be honored that God cares about our tears and stores
them up. Even more, He records them. They won't fall
unnoticed. You may cry in private over the challenges your
disability brings, but God sees you. And He's not impatient, hoping you'll pull it together. Every time you take
your tears to Him through prayer, the Lord will strengthen
you in that moment.

So cry out to the Father who sees and hears you. Let
Him be your source of strength and encouragement. For
you are not alone in your suffering. In fact, you matter so
much that God promises to see you in your most vulnerable moments.

God Understands a Heavy Heart

Jesus began to cry.
JOHN 11:35 CEB

· ·

Losing a pet is one of the hardest losses to manage because these fur babies are our constant companions. They love us no matter what we do, what we say, or whether we've showered. They run down the hallway to greet us when we come home. They snuggle up when we're sad and are ready to play at a moment's notice. And even more, they never smart off with snarky comebacks. Instead, they love us unconditionally.

Pour your heart out to God, sharing your grief with Him. He knows saying goodbye is hard because we've loved them deeply. He understands a heavy heart and has experienced grief too. In His great love and compassion, you will feel comforted. And as you think back on your beloved pet, God will be there to remember with you.

Loss of Power

Lord, show me your kindness and mercy, for these men oppose and oppress me all day long. Not a day goes by without somebody harassing me. So many in their pride trample me under their feet.

PSALM 56:1-2 TPT

Some people are just plain mean. They think it's funny to get us flustered. And while we may be able to banter with the best, theirs eventually crosses a line and becomes hurtful. Even when we ask them to stop, they continue. It doesn't seem to matter how we feel, and by the end of the day, we're angry and frustrated.

God is right there with you, ready to show kindness when asked. The world may try to beat you up, but the Lord will override their mean-spiritedness with His mercy. He will reverse their unkind words with His unwavering love. As you trust God, your oppressors will lose their power.

Walking Away from Dysfunctional Relationships

*What harm could man do to me? With God
on my side, I will not be afraid of what comes.
My heart overflows with praise to God and
for his promises. I will always trust in him.*

PSALM 56:11 TPT

. . . .

Sometimes the thought of ending a relationship is scary.
Our heart is torn even when we know walking away is
the right thing. We worry about untangling our lives from
someone, unsure how it might shake out. We're concerned
for any pushback that will make things even more unpleas-
ant. And while we see the need to make a break, we're
apprehensive.

God wants us thriving in healthy relationships, not
striving in dysfunctional ones. And when we feel holy
prompting to step away, our job is to trust and obey. We
don't need to worry about what may come, because the
Father promises to guide each step.

Adultery Is Never Justified

*Honor the sanctity of marriage and keep
your vows of purity to one another, for
God will judge sexual immorality in any
form, whether single or married.*
HEBREWS 13:4 TPT

Adultery—no matter how one may think it justified—is not honoring the covenant of marriage. It's not honoring God. And it brings with it a judgment before the Lord. Every day, we're all faced with countless temptations to step out of God's will for our marriage. From little white lies to speaking ill about our spouse to choosing adultery. But the blessings that come from respecting the commitment made are bountiful.

Keep your heart focused on God so you're strengthened to stay true to your husband. He authored marriage and will give you a beautiful one if you will both purpose to honor it. Without Him, you may not have the fortitude to forgo temptations.

But the Soul Lives

So I'm thanking you with all my heart,
with gratitude for all you've done. I will do
everything I've promised you, Lord. For you
have saved my soul from death and my feet
from stumbling so that I can walk before
the Lord bathed in his life-giving light.

PSALM 56:12–13 TPT

• •

As a believer, your soul is saved from death because salvation secured your place in heaven. You'll live forever in God's presence, but your body stays here. Scripture says we'll receive a new, glorified body once we enter the pearly gates. It won't suffer, age, or break down. So leaving our broken body here is a gift.

You may be facing death, but it's the loss of only your earthly frame. In a snap, your soul will ascend into heaven and live on. And the believers around you will be there soon too. Have hope! Take courage! Be thankful!

Walking by Faith through Foreclosure

*For we walk by faith [we regulate our lives
and conduct ourselves by our conviction or
belief respecting man's relationship to God
and divine things, with trust and holy fervor;
thus we walk] not by sight or appearance.*

2 CORINTHIANS 5:7 AMPC

So much of life these days requires us to trust God with holy fervor. We are urged to walk by faith—knowing God is in control—rather than let our circumstances guide our emotions and decisions. And if you're facing foreclosure, let today's verse inform your next steps carefully.

In our humanity, we are easily freaked out. The thought of losing a home feels insurmountable. And all kinds of fear and panic kick in and stir us up. But remembering God is on the throne and committing to trusting Him each step of the way will bring peace and comfort to your anxious heart.

What Is God's Plan for You?

Sarah's faith embraced God's miracle power to conceive even though she was barren and was past the age of childbearing, for the authority of her faith rested in the One who made the promise, and she tapped into his faithfulness.

HEBREWS 11:11 TPT

. . . .

Infertility isn't an issue for God. It doesn't confine Him or negate His powers. Just like the Lord made Sarah—a woman past childbearing years—fertile, if it's God's plan for you to have children, it will be.

The hard truth is that's not His plan for everyone. Some are meant to adopt children instead of having their own. Some are to be spiritual moms, loving those who need someone special to care. And for others, God's plan didn't include children at all. Let the Lord instill peace and understanding in your heart as you take your heartache to Him.

You Can Still Be Just

*But he's already made it plain how to live,
what to do, what GOD is looking for in men
and women. It's quite simple: Do what is fair
and just to your neighbor, be compassionate
and loyal in your love, and don't take
yourself too seriously—take God seriously.*

MICAH 6:8 MSG

The world may be unjust, but you can rise above the frustration and live with integrity toward others. You can choose to be fair in your dealings and reasonable in your relationships. You can be honest in your business affairs. And you can be objective and open-minded as you navigate life here on earth.

Your response to the injustice done to you doesn't need to be vengeful. Every day and in each circumstance, let your faith guide your actions. Be fair. Be compassionate and loyal. And be serious in your pursuit of righteous living, delighting God's heart.

The Sweetness of Slumber

*Now, because of you, Lord, I will lie down
in peace and sleep comes at once, for no
matter what happens, I will live unafraid!*
PSALM 4:8 TPT

Fear has a funny way of keeping us up at night. The day-time hours are busy with family and work, making it easy to put our worries on the back burner. But when the lights go out, it all catches up with us. Our head hits the pillow, and our mind starts playing our fears on a loop.

God wants us to release our concerns into His capable hands because doing so brings a supernatural peace to our heart. Once we realize we don't have to figure it all out, that God is already moving, we're able to rest and sleep. Knowing He's working all things for our good allows us to release the fear and embrace the sweetness of slumber.

Shifting Your Perspective

*Whatever you do, do it from the heart for
the Lord and not for people. You know
that you will receive an inheritance as a
reward. You serve the Lord Christ.*
COLOSSIANS 3:23–24 CEB

• •

One of the best ways to survive a stressful job is to shift
your perspective. It's hard to be excited to work with
those who create drama. But if you follow today's verse
and choose to honor God with your work, it takes trying
to please humanity out of the equation.

If you work to please the Lord, your integrity will also
impress those in authority over you. When you work with
a joyful spirit, your coworkers will respect your attitude.
Choosing to be positive instead of grumbling with the
gang will encourage others to follow. Do this from a heart
for God, and reap the blessings that come with it.

With You in Surgery

*When sickness comes, the Eternal is
beside them—to comfort them on their
sickbeds and restore them to health.*

PSALM 41:3 VOICE

. . . .

God loves you and is for you. He watches over and pro-
tects those who love Him. And through thick and thin, His
presence never strays from you. It's a constant force in
your life. So be confident, knowing that even in sickness
and surgery, the Lord is beside you always.

He's watching over the surgeon's hands. He's giving
wisdom to doctors for treatment protocols. God is direct-
ing each medication prescription with care. So you can
trust that when you're being wheeled into surgery and
the anesthesia begins to take effect, the Lord is standing
right there. Be comforted by this beautiful truth, and let it
bring peace and assurance that you are in the best hands
possible. . .*His.*

Subject Index

Scripture Index